Newto

Going Through the Motions to Stop Evil

Rocky Veach

ISBN-13: 978-0991229604 (IMN (In My Name))
ISBN-10: 0991229606

Newtown's Law
Going Through the Motions to Stop Evil

IMN (In My Name). A division of T.O.R.CH. Ministries
P.O. BOX 27
Southbury, CT 06488
www.rockyveach.com / www.rockyveach.org
rockyveach@gmail.com

ISBN-13: 978-0991229604 (IMN (In My Name))
ISBN-10: 0991229606

Editorial Consultants: Jordan Veach, Catherine Finlay Samose
Layout and Cover Design: Rachel Adams
Research Assistant: Molli Veach
Cover Image: Shutterstock, Image ID: 24697948, Copyright: Claudio Bertoloni

ENDORSEMENT

Rocky Veach is a friend and a true son in the faith. Because I KNOW him, I can wholeheartedly recommend his books to you. Look beyond the words, read between the lines and you will find the kind of treasure that shines through the heart of a man who has been touched by the heart of Jesus! God uses men but it is He Who calls people like you. He is raising up champions for His cause that will fight the good fight of faith and push back in the power of the Holy Spirit against any and every evil work the enemy seeks to perpetrate in towns and nations all over the world. Say yes to the Lord, and become an answer to the challenges around you in these crucial times. His message has always been a driving force, influencing masses of lost souls for heaven's sake. Let these pages help accelerate you into a fresh godly momentum that is beginning to sweep across planet earth again today!

Neil Miers, Founder, Global Connexions, www.neilmiers.com
President of COC International 1990-2010 Brisbane, Australia

DEDICATION

This book is dedicated to all those who respond to emergencies. Especially, those who gave their lives to save someone else. There is no greater example of love. Thank God for you!

I would also like to thank the faithful team of friends and associates who help me spread the Word. Bobbi, Rachel, Jordan, our staff at TORCH and Connections Church - you guys respond!

TABLE OF CONTENTS

ENDORSEMENT.. v

DEDICATION.. vii

TABLE OF CONTENTS............................…..… ix

CAUTION.. xi

FOREWARD...How Random is Your Reality?.............…........ xiii

CHAPTER 1…The End Starts At the Beginning…........... 1

CHAPTER 2…The Apple Doesn't Fall Far From the Tree.... 15

CHAPTER 3... 1st Move, We Haven't Been This Way Before.. 29

CHAPTER 4... 2nd Move, Head Games......................…....…… 43

CHAPTER 5... 3rd Move, The 1st Law Of Spiritual Motion..... 57

CHAPTER 6... 4th Move, The 2nd Law Of Spiritual Motion.... 75

CHAPTER 7.... 5th Move, The 3rd Law Of Spiritual Motion... 93

CHAPTER 8.... 6th Move, Making This Law Even Bigger...… 113

AFTERWORD...The Highest Law of All..................... 129

WORKS CITED..…... 137

OTHER RESOURCES...............…....................…... 141

CAUTION:
This Book Will Change Your Life, But Why Wait?
MAKE THE MOST IMPORTANT DECISION OF YOUR LIFE NOW!

If you do not believe in Jesus Christ and have a sincere heart toward following Him, Newtown's Law may not mean as much to you. It will still be in effect, but often even working against you and those you love, just beyond your perception of everyday reality!

Therefore, I must recommend that you let the only One Who is truly "good" save you BEFORE learning what you can do about evil. In fact, he Bible teaches that it is only with good that we can overcome evil! This is not the easiest decision to make and requires courage but why not start the process by kicking evil out of your own life?

The Bible says we must all believe in our heart that God raised Jesus from the dead and confess with our mouths that He is Lord (Romans 10:9-10). It is in the doing of both things that we are saved. God desires a personal relationship with you but he also demands a public recommendation from you! If you are willing to do both, it proves you are serious. If not, you probably won't be willing to accept the full invitation of Jesus to "FOLLOW" Him.

Take the time to consider what is being asked of you. A Christian is called to break with the past and go forward into God's future. This requires "repenting" or turning away from sin and then receiving the pardon Jesus died on the cross to purchase for you. Salvation is costly because it is precious. The eternal rewards are great. Not only are you saved from the unending punishment of hell but more importantly you are destined to spend forever in a heavenly state of being that will begin once you make your decision!

So, before moving further, whether you are unsaved or simply not in a right place with God, stop and ask Jesus to forgive you right now and become the Lord of your life. Then take up your cross and begin following Him. Now, you are prepared to "do something about it!"

FOREWORD

HOW RANDOM IS YOUR REALITY?

What are the odds that a pastor would have a church in Littleton, Colorado, during the Columbine High School shootings and then find himself in Newtown, Connecticut, when the Sandy Hook Elementary School tragedy happened 13½ years later? Believe it or not, that is my bizarre story. The unique perspective it affords me, can help others build the kind of spiritual preparedness this dangerous era continues to demand from all of us.

Although there have been so many loving, brave, and generous responses to the people affected by the outbreak of evil, especially here in the United States over this past decade, many still feel helpless in its wake. Deep within them, people tend to think that there must be an underlying 'cause' to these kinds of 'effects'. Human beings tend to know when there is something unknown lurking beneath the surface of a situation but most are uncertain as to why they feel that way. This is why questions like, *Why do bad things happen to good people?* and *How could something like this happen in my town?* are so often asked.

If my experience is any indicator, even the most seemingly random things probably are not happening by accident. This book is not, however, really about my experience. It is more about what someone in my shoes should take away from it to help give others a more substantial plan of action. The fact is that many mathematicians and physicists argue that nothing is truly random. To them, everything is a product of cause and effect on some level. After going through a couple of these 'random' incidents first hand, I have started to realize how much more biblical this opinion is than many innocent bystanders like me, may understand.

A friend told me recently about an interview he had watched on TV, where a spokesman for a government investigation agency explained how coincidence does not factor into his organization's approach to solving crime. Instead he said everything in an investigation is looked at as fact, leading to a result. This is one of the biggest secrets to their incredible success at catching the most elusive criminals. To understand life's most difficult circumstances and really do something about them, we have to look at the spiritual side of things this same factual way. That is, we want to learn to think like God through these situations.

The Bible clearly teaches that tragedy, as we experience it here on earth, doesn't just happen. It originates from the interaction between mankind and an opposing force, Satan. It's not a popular message today, but neither good nor evil are impersonal forces. They are persons, locked in a cosmic battle that affects even the most innocent bystanders, as Newtown so sadly proved. Satan has always been a big problem. Jesus Christ has always been the bigger answer. Christians have to stand up with His authority in the midst of an 'evil day' with the power to expose the cause behind the heinous crimes being loosed in society. We have become easy targets because of our own ignorance of spiritual warfare. It has caused us to stop confronting the person of Satan, responsible for such otherwise unexplainable troubles.

Once the negative source of evil is recognized and how it operates is understood, people can choose to apply God's positive counter-force to overcome the attacks and change the effects. The more His people get united around what Jesus says about any given situation, the more power they will have to swing the momentum in a direction reflective of God's will. The Bible is filled with examples of this clash of spiritual motion, but I'm afraid modern mainstream believers who have experienced very little persecution or discomforts have forgotten how overcoming the odds really work. God's Word contains a principle that could be termed the 'Law of Spiritual Motion' which teaches us how to eventually always trump chaos and calamity.

Therefore the title <u>Newtown's Law</u>, is meant to highlight this serious scriptural principle through a play on words. As I was discussing this project with my daughter Jordan, the term 'Newtown's Law' just kind of popped out of her mouth with that familiar undertone that tells you, *this is what needs to be said*. If you remember Sir Isaac Newton's laws of motion, you will understand the importance of universal laws and how motion plays a key role in the outcome of two colliding forces, regardless of whether those experiencing their effects realize they are at work or not. Objects respond according to the equations by which they are governed. They are callous facts, which continue to create results, good or bad, irrespective of our belief, involvement, or mood.

However, it takes someone like Newton to discover such realities before others can begin to unravel the mysteries behind many of the physical consequences they face. Other people's time and energy can then be used to discover, according to the laws at work around them, even greater blessings for the human race. When Newton saw an apple fall from a tree, it turned out to reveal more than just how we could avoid being hit by falling objects. It also created opportunities for inventors like the Wright brothers to reverse the same law and fly the first airplane a couple of hundred years later.

Spiritually speaking, it seems that we have to rediscover the most important facts about God via the stories about and teachings of the Abrahams, Josephs, Moses, Davids, Daniels, Peters and Pauls written in our Bible. Scripture is full of character sketches detailing how those who discovered God used their revelation to help others overcome the negative forces they faced in life. History also records the exploits of people just like you and me who have known the Lord and turned their heavenly discoveries into future blessings for many in this world. The spiritual law outlined in the following chapters can literally help you to become someone 'in the know' with God, another answer for so many people caught in the tragedy and trauma of today's world. My prayer is that you will become an important part of His force to be reckoned with, in this era of spiritual warfare that we find ourselves in.

How I Got to Newtown

Like many people, I often struggle to hear from God about the things I want to know. He does however, have a history of speaking to me about the strangest things when I least expect them. This being true, I usually feel completely unqualified to do anything about them at the time. Like, for example, when He woke me up at 5 a.m. on Thursday, April 20, 2000 and gave me a message which has served as a theme for my ministry. He said, "Rocky, tell my people I want to be their Jonathan!" It was a strange word with even stranger timing—exactly one year after the Columbine High School shootings in Littleton, Colorado, where I had lived and ministered.

Later, in the summer of 2006, as I was preparing to move my family from Colorado to southeastern New York State to minister to a needy church, the Lord woke me up again, this time from a Saturday afternoon nap, with another startling statement. "Go to Newtown," is all He said but how He said it was what really got my attention. There is an internally audible way the Holy Spirit speaks that can make you think that everyone else around you must have also heard Him. Like the message in this book, this second experience was urgent. Little did I realize at the time how it would apply six years later and how I would come to understand that it was directly connected to the word that I received six years before.

As we will soon see, things don't just happen. To make a long story short, I eventually ended up in Newtown, Connecticut after having lived in New York. It was January of 2012 when our church plant began meeting in the town's historic, Edmond Town Hall. Once we finally got there, it had been such an unusual journey that I almost questioned the validity of the whole experience. That changed in December of that year, when it became much more obvious why the Lord had dropped this far away little town onto my spiritual radar, so far in advance.

I have learned by experience that when God speaks to you loudly and openly, it is probably because you are going to need to remember what He said every step of the way toward His will for your life. I believe the tragic event that unfolded in the Sandy Hook section of Newtown that December, is an important indicator for all of America that something insidious has been happening on this generation's watch, and that we must now decide to confront it. An era of evil that started with Columbine, (and has repeated itself over thirty more times in schools throughout this country) erupted in Newtown with the sound of a final warning that something wicked was intent on imposing a 'new normal' in our culture.

The good news is that God is never unprepared. His heart is broken, but His love for His people dictates that He always has a greater response. This means He also has His spiritual responders ready ahead of time, just as emergency management agencies have physical response teams waiting for every next, but yet unknown, crisis we will face. As Jonathan equipped David for the call on His life, so the Lord prepares us ahead of time to be the answer others will need (1 Samuel 18:1-5).

In the midst of this horror in Newtown, I suddenly realized how my life was a reflection of this inexhaustible determination in the mind of God to deal with evil. If He alerts someone like me more than 13 years in advance and then sends me six years ahead of the event to where it will happen when I have no idea what He is talking about, what else does He have up His sleeve?
God knows the solution long before we know what needs a solution. He is more tired of seeing America kill its own children than I am. Joseph's life in the Bible was an illustration of Jesus, God's Son and the world's Savior. It teaches us clearly that what has been meant for evil, He is always intent on reversing for good. Not only is there a way to do something about it—He *is* the way! I have written this book to help remind Christians of their authority in Christ and their responsibility to show up on behalf of Him for the lost, hurting, and victimized people of this world.

This mini-book is a rally cry with a mega-message to remind you just how brave you really can be in the Lord. Read it and respond to the revelation you find within these pages. I believe something good awaits you here, something God may say loudly today as a means of sending you somewhere important as part of His answer to someone else's future.

CHAPTER ONE

THE END STARTS AT THE BEGINNING

If a part of any equation is left out, it is nearly impossible to find the accurate solution. This is one reason why there are so many coincidences in life. When we haven't yet considered all available information, we usually do not realize it. To solve the cycle of 'random' violence that we face today, we might want to take into account the 'God factor'. The Bible has no problem telling us He is *the* answer from the very beginning.

Most people have heard the term, Alpha and Omega, the first and last letters of the Greek alphabet, as Jesus describes Himself in Revelation (Revelation.1:8, 11). These words are used in the writings of the New Testament to describe God as 'the beginning' and 'the end', just before we are given His graphic illustration of the end of time. But have you considered the Hebrew language of Genesis 1:1? This language makes everything in life just a little more solvable.

The fourth word found in the Bible does not even translate into English because there is no suitable equivalent for it. God arranged for two letters, aleph and tav, which are the same as alpha and omega, to be situated just after His name in the very first verse of scripture. 'Et', as it is pronounced, is sometimes known as a binding word in Hebrew. How interesting that God identifies Himself as not only the Creator of all things but more importantly, the beginning and end of everything before there was a beginning or end to anything. This is also why Jesus reiterates these same terms at the end of scripture. The verse can also mean God is not only the beginning and the end but everything in between. [*Lost in Translation, Rediscovering the Roots of the Hebrew Faith* by John Klein and Adam Spears, Selah Publishing Group, LLC, Tennessee, Pages 23 and 24]

There is an answer to everything, this tells us that the answer is a *someone.* If there is no God and we are all on our own, then why do we care so much? We care because He is real and He *is* the solution for even our most difficult problems. We need to stop wasting so much time and effort asking the wrong kinds of questions. Those questions can only lead to short-term solutions anyway, because they leave Him out of the equation. The most dangerous situations demand that we ask ourselves, *What does God say about this and what does He want me to do about it?*

Answer the Questions to Get the Answer

We have all noticed that bad things happen to good people a lot more often when good people do nothing about evil. Modern society does very little about evil daily yet still asks the age-old question that immediately follows tragedy...why? I'm pretty sure the kids of tomorrow will one day ask why we didn't do more than ask questions that keep people from getting real answers. They will want us to have combed through all the emotions of grief until we finally ask the more concrete question, 'what now'?

'Why' doesn't normally help us find lasting answers until it brings us back to the original 'what happened?' that we experienced when the bad news first shocked us into a new awareness of real and present danger. 'Why' is important but only as a first question leading to the final answer. 'What actually happened' also says 'let's do something to prevent this from happening again.' It helps us get into position to bring triumph out of the tragedies we face in life.

I certainly did not ask for the perspective God has given me but maybe it allows me to identify a blind-spot in our culture and help provide the spiritual answer many do not know they need when addressing evil. When people around Sandy Hook discovered my family and I had also lived near Columbine, their almost automatic first question was, "Why were you in both places?" The two most offered answers by the same people to their own question reveal the point I am trying to make. One group naturally thought, "What is wrong with you...maybe I shouldn't stand so close!" While the second concluded, without prior suggestion that I must have been there for a higher purpose.

Maybe you had one of those same initial reactions. So, let me turn the tables and ask you, 'Why?' We can all get caught in a repetitive cycle of behavior when we simply do not process the information necessary to escape the cycle. These questions I received explain our inherent tendency to want to know why and to question things we usually aren't interested in doing anything about. In my case, I noticed that very few of those same people really wanted to continue the dialogue long enough to find out what may have made me so 'dangerous'. They also didn't come to our town-wide prayer meetings to seek answers or help me with the 'divine mission' they so readily assumed I had been given.

These are unusual times, but even in a place where innocent lives had just been lost, people were mostly just talking...the same thing we all do on some level, especially when we are nervous and unsure of the 'whys.' It is an alternative form of taking action, which helps us feel better about things we can't control, while tricking us into thinking we've done enough about them. What about you? I will tell you that there are real answers, but the real question is: are you willing to be responsible for what finding an answer may require of you?

This second, first-hand experience as a citizen, neighbor and pastor in the aftermath of school shootings has brought me to terms with a truth that only frustrated me the first time I went through it. We don't need answers as much as we need to do the right things with the answers that we have. As I said in the Foreword of this book, coincidences tend to have a basis in fact if you look long and hard enough. I didn't just happen to have a church in Newtown, Connecticut. I was supposed to be there as part of an answer. Not because of something good or bad about me, but maybe just to help simply identify good and bad.

Instead of asking, "Why do bad things happen to good people?"

try answering that question with "For the same reason good things happen to bad people." Give it a minute or a month, I promise it will start to make sense. This is because that question leaves God out of the equation or at best, only leaves the door open to Him as being one possible solution. The answer removes Him as our problem when we encounter most forms of trouble and restores Him to His proper place of loving Father, fair Judge, and equal-opportunity Creator.

After thirty years of studying scripture and walking with God, I can assure you that in those rare times where God is standing directly in our path, things are far worse on that path than we realize. People usually are so hardened at that point they no longer want Him to be their answer. We are close to that in this country, but there is still hope. Remembering that good is who God really is will be the ultimate key to recovery in the midst of tragic circumstances. See Psalms 37 and 73.

Confusing Opposites Creates Opposition

If you pay close enough attention to what is going on around you, the Bible promises that something within you will find points of faith that lead to the conclusion that God is the Creator. Knowing that God is the Creator will inevitably be followed by the knowledge of another obvious fact—something or *someone* else has been working overtime to destroy all the best things that God has made. The many opposites in life naturally define themselves by identifying their counterparts. For instance, hot and cold, big and small, up and down, light and dark, true and false, right and wrong, new and old, fact and fiction, sickness and health, plus and minus, heaven and hell, God and Satan are all opposites that are so contrary to one another that we just kind of know, in a general sense, what one is once we have experienced the other. We have a built-in sense about these things that make it nearly impossible to confuse what these terms and their opposites, mean to us. To confuse these opposing terms creates the kind of confusion that breeds chaos and naturally begs the question, 'Why?'

"What sorrow for those who say that evil is good and good is evil, that dark is light and light is dark, that bitter is sweet and sweet is bitter." **Isaiah 5:20 NLT**

This is the reason evil is a crime everywhere. We all 'just know' it isn't good. Our sense of God's goodness and His righteousness tell us that evil is inherently wrong. So, even when wrong is intentionally called right by others, and especially when otherwise 'good people' don't want to get involved in the uncomfortable process of calling it out, the very presence of evil works against itself. We all know evil is a bully. It has an intimidating way about it—threatening to "get us" if we say or do anything about it, but its own warped nature ultimately serves as its downfall. Evil is a sick spiritual disease that can't help but expose the existence of something better: its age-old counterpart and the greater force known as 'good.' Although it often seems like nobody wants to see evil in its infancy, everyone can see it once the pillage and plunder of the worst kind of bad has blown through a life, community, or nation.

Thankfully, all human beings have this thing called a 'conscience' to help them see evil coming and to motivate them to do something about it before it has had time to spread. Serving as an inner surveillance system, this conduit between the spirit and soul of man is intended to make us 'conscious' of things that are not right in life. When something morally wrong is lurking in our backyards, our conscience detects the intrusion and alerts us to the need for action. The Greek language of the New Testament defines conscience as co-perception, a mechanism placed within us to help us see more completely. God has equipped us to distinguish between the opposites we will face in life, especially given the fact that we are created in His image to deal with physical and mental realities from His spiritual vantage point.

The beauty of this God-given inner indicator however, is not just its amazing ability to sense what is bad or wrong. The fact that it automatically performs that function only demonstrates, once again, the reality of something far more important—right and good. However, it is what we are required to *do* once we *know* that is the hard part. This is where people get stuck and it is why we keep repeating Newtown-like tragedies all across America. Knowing what is good is a natural inclination but choosing to understand the workings of evil is not. At some point we have to find the courage to finish the task that keeps presenting itself to us in this country. We have to overcome evil with the good we know instead of just holding each other's hands, loving people through the difficult times, and hoping it doesn't happen again. As of the time of this writing 'it' has already happened again.

"Remember, it is sin to know what you ought to do and then not do it." **James 4:17 NLT**

"Don't let evil conquer you, but conquer evil by doing good." **Romans 12:21 NLT**

We don't have to look too far into the past or too far around us to find corroborating evidence for what is worst about our human nature, warning us not to allow it to go unchecked in our lives or society at large. You know, those places and times where law has been so compromised, politics so corrupted, the truth so covered up, and good so disguised, that people are no longer willing to do anything about what is worst in and around them. When other people confuse opposites, they naturally create environments which resonate loudly around us. The mere names of diabolical figures from our past make us want to reverse their wrongs and act against evil before it arrives uninvited at our own doorsteps. Unfortunately, the reason such people are so stuck in our conscious awareness is because society, at those respective times, let them go way too far before finding the courage to do anything about them.

Life experience teaches us if we play with fire, we are going to get burned. When we do get burned, what's the first thing we look for? Something cold! World history teaches us when we know what is good yet choose to wink at evil, even in its lesser forms, there is always a future appointment with the consequences. If we neglect to stand up for what is right, there is usually someone else, somewhere else, waiting to pay a portion of the price for our neglect. Unless someone has revised your facts surrounding the details of World War II, there are some people still alive today suffering from the mere memories created by the sins of those who did nothing about the earliest indicators of Adolf Hitler's hidden agenda. As long as we keep such world events fresh in our minds, we will naturally look for exactly the opposite in our living environments—something good, something God.

"Beloved, do not imitate evil, but imitate good. He who does good is of God; he who does evil has not seen (discerned or experienced) God [has enjoyed no vision of Him and does not know Him at all]." **3 John 11 AMP**

Places like Newtown demand that we deal with opposites, especially if we find ourselves calloused enough to not want to get to the bottom of what is killing the most innocent, and not coincidentally, the most God-like citizens of our country. The heinousness of crimes like the one committed in Newtown, should force us right up to an unforeseen moral point-of-no-return and then make us feel the responsibility to push past it. The problem today is that we aren't *feeling* like we should be because we haven't listened to our deepest indicators. If we want to solve the mystery of evil plaguing the conscience of our nation, we'd better start listening to our own consciences again! Here is the key: as much as we all possess that inner knowing when something is wrong either in or around us, we also know we don't really want to know any more about evil than we have to.

Evil is a scary subject—one that most of us inherently fear carries an ability to suck us into its dark clutches if we get too close. More than just one of those cognitive bias brain blind spots we find interesting in psychology class, current events today are proving that evil works just as comfortably on our playgrounds as it does in our well-loved horror films. By not dealing with our opposing circumstances correctly, we have unleashed the wrong kind of opposition in the places we suspected it least. It has jumped all the way from the big screen to the classroom and we seem to be contently living with it.

After personally living in two of the 31 different communities where school shootings have occurred in the United States during a span of thirteen years, it is completely clear to me that innocent children have increasingly become a major modern target of our past attitudes toward evil and that someone has to do something more than is currently being done about it. No one wants to confront the snake on our playground but everyone expects to keep playing in a venom-free environment. Not knowing would be dangerous, not wanting to know is deadly. It seems that we live in an era where the sins of fathers are quite literally and rapidly passing down to their children and we better do something a little more serious about it.

"In the future, when you have children and grandchildren...do not corrupt yourselves by making idols of any kind. This is evil in the sight of the Lord your God and will arouse his anger...You must not bow down to them or worship them, for I, the Lord your God, am a jealous God who will not tolerate your affection for any other gods. I lay the sins of the parents upon their children; the entire family is affected, even children in the third and fourth generations of those who reject me."
Deuteronomy 4:25 and 5:9 NLT

According to the Bible, we can sometimes be dealing with issues today that are rooted so far into yesterday that we have no understanding of why they can be happening. This is especially true when it comes to playing with what God calls evil. If we do, it can break out later when we least expect it. It is no wonder civil authorities today often have no real answers for the worst crimes society faces. God has the answers, because He understands the spiritual process going on behind the physical events. Christians should also have the answers because they know God, but they really don't today for the most part because they have stopped staying informed about His ideas on these subjects. If there is a creation there is a Creator. If there is destruction there is also a destroyer.

Go Back to the Beginning

Our biggest problem is that we keep thinking like Eve did in the Garden of Eden. We're unsure whether God Himself is the problem or the answer. Consequently, good and evil aren't clear to us today. They aren't going to be either, until we look back *to* God instead of *at* what our subtly deceptive and often painful circumstances seem to tell us about Him.

In order to make sense of senseless circumstances and regain our spiritual bearings in life, we need an old-fashioned Sunday school refresher course. (I say old-fashioned because most Christians today do not attend regular church meetings, much less anything extra that might teach them to know the things about God and man we are discussing here.) Once common Bible knowledge unfortunately is not so common anymore. This is why we tend to do things like blame God for the works of the devil and vice-versa. Good and evil aren't clear because the persons behind their operation have become confused.

What we need to do is simply go back to the beginning and work forward from there. "Genesis" is the first book in the Bible. The word itself means origin or source and its contents can help us back up to see the bigger picture and remember where things came from when we lose sight of 'why' due to our difficulties. Two very important concepts are found in Genesis. First, God is the creator. As I said before, this should be obvious just by looking around at the intelligent design of creation, but we have a tendency to not believe the most logical things. Romans 1:18-25 is very clear about how we all got into this position:

"But God shows his anger from heaven against all sinful,

wicked people who suppress the truth by their wickedness. They know the truth about God because he has made it obvious to them. For ever since the world was created, people have seen the earth and sky. Through everything God made, they can clearly see his invisible qualities, his eternal power and divine nature. So they have no excuse for not knowing God. Yes, they knew God, but they wouldn't worship him as God or even give him thanks. And they began to think up foolish ideas of what God was like. As a result, their minds became dark and confused. Claiming to be wise, they instead became utter fools. And instead of worshiping the glorious, ever-living God, they worshiped idols made to look like mere people and birds and animals and reptiles. So God abandoned them to do whatever shameful things their hearts desired. As a result, they did vile and degrading things with each other's bodies. They traded the truth about God for a lie. So they worshiped and served the things God created instead of the Creator himself, who is worthy of eternal praise! Amen."
Romans 1:18-25 NLT

God does get angry and when He does, there has always been a good reason for it. We also discover in the New Testament this second *someone* in the world equation who consistently seeks to exacerbate our sinfulness and use it as a release point for his own brand of evil, as he places it into the human narrative. We fail to find real answers when we only follow our human instincts at the expense of simple faith. Once we wreck the spiritual climate that God created for us to live in, almost anything goes. Romans 16:17-20 is clear about who is responsible for using our irresponsibility where good is concerned for the furtherance of his own evil purposes:

"Watch out for people who cause divisions and upset people's faith by teaching things contrary to what you have been taught. Stay away from them. Such people are not serving Christ our Lord; they are serving their own personal interests. By smooth talk and glowing words they deceive innocent

people. But everyone knows that you are obedient to the Lord. This makes me very happy. I want you to be wise in doing right (good) and to stay innocent of any wrong (evil). The God of peace will soon crush Satan under your feet..."
Romans 16:17-20 NLT

Now, back to Genesis. Notice there were also two especially important trees located in the center of Eden. One was **The Tree of Life.** The one that would become of even more 'central' importance to those who lived there however, was called, **The Tree of the Knowledge of Good and Evil** (Genesis 2:17; 3:22). Adam and Eve were forbidden to eat from this second tree while living in the supernatural state they were originally created in. How interesting that we once wanted to know about good and evil so much that we were willing to deal with the unknown consequences and now we don't want to know any more than we absolutely have to. We lost the garden but there's still a snake loose in the world who doesn't want anyone to know how God gave His Son on a *tree that gives us life.*

Humanity was obviously meant to walk "in the image of God" by experiencing heaven-on-earth living conditions. All of us dream of the utopian lifestyle that was snatched away from mankind by the sin of Adam and Eve, and would not be completely found again until Jesus (the second Adam), reappeared. On Calvary, by dying on the cross, Jesus completed the process of restoring mankind. Heaven and earth will be seamlessly reattached when Jesus returns. It will be physically as it now is spiritually in those who follow Jesus Christ with their heart and soul.

Even the history of the meaning of the word *utopia* tells us how people have long understood that paradise on earth is only possible when sustained by the spiritual power of God's presence. When Sir Thomas More first coined the word in 1516 from the Greek *ou-topos*, meaning 'no place', he was using it as a play on words, as the similar *eu-topos* means 'a good place'. So, it would seem that More was saying that the perfect place exists nowhere. This has been true

11

on this planet since the events described in Genesis. Utopia only existed physically when the absence of sin opened parallel spiritual doorways to the presence of God, and before Satan introduced sin, opening those same kinds of doors to himself. Maybe you remember these famously fatal words voiced by not just the shrewdest animal in God's garden but, and more importantly, by the even subtler spirit inspiring its thoughts.

"'Did God really say you must not eat the fruit from any of the trees in the garden?...You won't die!' the serpent replied to the woman. 'God knows that your eyes will be opened as soon as you eat it, and you will be like God, knowing both good and evil.'" Genesis 3:1, 4-5 NLT

Now notice how similar, yet different God's own words were:

"Then the Lord God said, 'Look, the human beings have become like us, knowing both good and evil. What if they reach out, take fruit from the tree of life, and eat it? Then they will live forever!'" Genesis 3:22 NLT

Again, there are reasons for everything. Some reasons we need to know and some we are better off if we don't know. This is one we need to know if we are going to do something about the increasing *random* violence that seems to keep cropping up in similar fashion. Just like creation, there is another intelligent design behind destruction. The cosmic battleground has come to our very doorstep today. The opposing forces are those who follow God and those who follow Satan. The principles are Good and Evil. The stakes are Life and Death.

Newtown serves as more than just another reminder that we must deal bravely in the aftermath of shocking crimes. It reveals roots to our problems so dark and deep that the only answer left is God. If we will let the Bible put the D back in evil, we can begin to realize that it is not the simple 'what' that we're facing today, but the much more sinister 'who.' Only from that vantage point can we start to do something about the evil, because it enables us to realize that God has already done something about him. The solution for dealing with the perpetrator of evil is found in surrendering our services to Him who is good.

"The name of the Lord is a strong tower, the [consistently] righteous man [upright and in right standing with God] runs into it and is safe, high [above evil] and strong." **Proverbs 18:10 AMP**

"For the Scriptures say, '"As surely as I live,' says the Lord, 'every knee will bend to me, and every tongue will confess and give praise to God.'" **Romans 4:11 NLT**

"For He has rescued us from the kingdom of darkness and transferred us into the Kingdom of His dear Son,..." **Colossians 2:13**

"Therefore, God elevated him to the place of highest honor and gave him the name above all other names, that at the name of Jesus every knee should bow, in heaven and on earth and under the earth, and every tongue confess that Jesus Christ is Lord, to the glory of God the Father." **Philippians 2:9-11 NLT**

I am banking on the fact that you, like me, are here for a reason. You are no random coincidence. Jesus gave His life to transfer you back to where you once belonged. He triumphed completely over Satan and in that process, through our identification with Him, you and I are His solution for the evil around us. The Lord always obeyed God's word as He moved forward in His assignment to restore mankind. Now Satan has to move for those who follow in the motion of the One who has already mastered him!

CHAPTER TWO

THE APPLE DOESN'T FALL FAR FROM THE TREE

We need Newton's apple to drop, again. I think God used the world's most famous fruit to reveal the truth of motion to Isaac Newton for a reason. How coincidental could it really be that the same fruit many assume Satan used to seduce Eve into falling in Eden, is exactly what fell off a tree in England several thousand years later at another critical moment in human history? The first incident tricked people into thinking for themselves apart from God and created a downward spiral for the entire race. In the second case a believer searching for deeper meaning, saw something that sparked his thinking and led to a renewed understanding of motion and renewed forward progress through technology. Newton's 'Law of Motion' was a reminder to the entire world that something bigger is always going on as opposed to what just seems obvious.

It sounds suspiciously like God wanted to rattle our collective noggin and get our spiritual attention. Newton's discovery of the way motion worked, identified how a few previously unknown elements could combine in the universe to define why things often happen the way they do. It must have been an eye-opening revelation to the people of his time, how many of the seemingly random things in life had been operating according to a higher procedure the whole time! I wonder if we don't need a similar revelation today, even though we live in the heights of the technological advancements resulting from that era. Could there be simple answers for some of the spiritual problems that we face? Maybe, as in the case of Isaac Newton, answers have been dropping all around us, but we haven't looked into the obvious deeply enough to understand what continues to be obscure to so many.

NEWTON'S LAW

In researching the Law of Motion, I happened to notice that the name Newton is merely a contraction for Newtown. Like the truth in this book, it was obvious yet obscured from my understanding simply because I had not had any reason to consider it before. Now that I had reason, it seemed time for me to get serious about finding out what it was about Newton's work that might help provide a context for revealing some, otherwise obscure truths that God wants exposed to a new generation. What I learned has been obvious all the time, yet we probably have not thought much about it, even though we need to understand it now more than ever. We need to refresh ourselves in God's basic spiritual laws so that we can lift our circumstances above the gravity of the tragic problems mankind is facing in life today.

Let's briefly reconsider Isaac Newton's most famous discovery. This overall Law of Motion is actually made up of three laws working together. Again, the mechanics of these describe what is constantly going on in the world around us, usually beyond the plane of our conscious awareness. We will come back to them in detail. For now, simply look at their definitions:

Newton's 1st Law (The Law of Inertia): *A body remains at rest or in uniform motion in a straight line unless acted upon by a force.*

Newton's 2nd Law: *A body's rate of change of momentum is proportional to the force causing it.*

Newton's 3rd Law: *When a force acts on a body due to another body then an equal and opposite force acts simultaneously on that body.*

(Source: Collins English Dictionary)

Unless you are physicist or currently enrolled and excelling in a physics class somewhere, you will immediately notice how difficult these definitions are to wrap your head around. Most of the other scientists during Newton's own time rejected the theory themselves because it is so counterintuitive. They just don't make much sense to us until we put them into the context of our own practical reality. Nevertheless, they accurately describe the very true and present reality, of which, we are only one small part.

To help us get back in touch, let's put these laws into everyday terms. For example, the first law is the real reason that you should always wear a seatbelt inside your car. The second law tells us why it has to be fastened securely. The third law reveals how badly we stand to get hurt if we don't do either. Of course, Isaac Newton had no car to drive. He went to all of this verbiage simply to describe why an apple falls to the ground. Honestly, most of us would rather just pick it up and eat it before the 'five-second rule' went into effect. Who knew that one answer from God about the way He designed things to move scientifically, could unlock the answers to so many of life's other unresolved issues?

Today, it might be easier to look at a Newton's Cradle device—you know, that funky little conversation piece that someone gave you for Christmas once upon a time? Before I was saved, some people in my hometown called it a set of 'knockers' but we obviously had the wrong idea of the principles it displayed. This reminds me of modern Christianity in that it was a lot of fun using the device incorrectly, right up until the parts got tangled up and they had to throw the whole thing away. Even though you may have seen this device and many have even understood the laws of motion it portrayed, you probably had no idea it could one day serve to remind you of how to help restore positive momentum in your increasingly negative world. (To see this device refer to the cover of this book. To see it working, go to http://en.wikipedia.org/wiki/Wikipedia:Featured_picture_candidates/Newton's_Cradle.)

Ohio State University's website describes the lesson that we can learn from this device as follows:

"Newton's First Law, the Law of Inertia, states that an object at rest will remain at rest and an object in motion will remain in motion, unless acted upon by an outside force. The ball that is pulled back and released wants to keep moving, and the stationary balls would like to remain motionless. The collision that takes place between the moving ball and the stationary balls result in force acting upon all the balls in the system. The moving ball has a certain amount of momentum (a tendency to remain in motion) and when it is stopped by the collision, this momentum is transferred to the next ball in the line. The next ball cannot go anywhere since it is sandwiched, so it transfers the momentum to the next ball in line. This transfer of momentum continues until the momentum is given to the last ball in the line. Because its movement is not blocked, when the last ball receives the momentum it continues on the path of the first ball. This process will repeat itself, going back and forth, until the energy of the system is lost to air resistance, friction and vibrations and all the balls again come to rest. When two balls are pulled back and released then two balls at the opposite end will move. This is the result, rather than one ball moving with twice the momentum, because both momentum and energy must be conserved. The only way to satisfy that condition is if the same number of balls are ejected as were hit. Newton's third Law, which states that for every action there is an equal and opposite reaction, can be observed by the motion of the Newtown's Cradle system."

Adam's Cradle, How Civilization Was Rocked

Now, if we check our Bibles, like Sir Isaac was also famous for doing, we will find something very interesting regarding good and evil in connection with motion in the real history of the cradle of civilization. Motion is such an important concept in the creation of the universe that we find it in the second verse of the Bible:

"IN THE beginning God (prepared, formed, fashioned) created the heavens and the earth. [Hebrews 11:3] The earth was without form and an empty waste, and darkness was upon the face of the very great deep. The spirit of God was MOVING (hovering, brooding) over the face of the waters. And God said..." **Genesis 1:1-3a AMP**

The word 'moving' in Hebrew is used here and in two other verses in the Old Testament. In Deuteronomy 32:11, it describes the way an eagle flutters over her brood in the nest as she prepares them to fly for the first time. This particular verse is part of a song Moses sang, giving the Israelites an illustration of how God, in His goodness, had worked with them personally to deliver them from the evils of Egypt and restore His blessing to them. Again in Jeremiah 23:9, it refers to the prophet lamenting the fact that his heart is broken and his bones shake because of the sins of Israel and in particular, the wickedness of the prophets and priests themselves because they had brought evil upon the whole land.

In one Bible word, we can begin to see a kind of spiritual law of motion. Things happen a certain way starting with the movements of God, creating reactions not only in heavenly dimensions, but here on earth among people who, though they are very human, are also quite spiritual, being created in the image of God Himself. Scripture actually teaches that everything physical bears the reflection of that which is spiritual because of this same principle.

"By faith we understand that the entire universe was formed at God's command, that what we now see did not come from anything that can be seen." **Hebrews 11:3 NLT**

"For ever since the world was created, people have seen the earth and sky. Through everything God made, they can clearly see his invisible qualities—his eternal power and divine nature. So they have no excuse for not knowing God" **Romans 1:20 NLT**

Earthly things are the creation of a Heavenly Father. Therefore, natural and supernatural were never meant to be, and can never actually be completely separated. Notice how, like the ordered movements of a Newton's Cradle, God's original move as Creator of everything in this new order, produced a reaction of blessing and complete goodness. Man was the greatest of the good things created, to whom was given the direct blessing of absolute success in ruling over the rest of the creatures in this natural kingdom God had made.

"And God blessed them and said to them, 'Be fruitful, multiply, and fill the earth, and subdue it [using all its vast resources in the service of God and man]; and have dominion over the fish in the sea, the birds of the air, and over every living creature that moves upon the earth'." **Genesis 1:29 AMP**

As we shall see through the initiation of another spiritual movement, the physical dimension has been corrupted. Both Satan and Jesus followed its laws, where the desire to effect mankind was concerned. When God made Adam and Eve, He directed them in the ways that they should move. When Satan wanted to corrupt them, he simply moved toward them in a deceptive attempt to project their thoughts in a direction away from God's will.

If Satan could move them mentally toward the tree of the knowledge of good and evil, just enough to get them to taste its fruit, he knew that they would take it from there. Not only would they be forced off God's original intended spiritual course for them, but even worse, their actions would dictate the momentum of the natural world around them, right into Satan's own evil clutches. His strategy was to tempt them to move outside of God's expressed or known directives by themselves, through the use of their own willpower. Fast forward six thousand or so years later and now you know the *what* behind the *why* in regard to evil being so prevalent in your world.

Now, in this little book, I am not going to solve any of the spiritual mysteries that God has reserved for other places and times. I will not put a dent in the amount of unknown mysteries of His amazing universe. I am certainly not even trying to make a scientific correlation between Newton's Laws and the higher truths often hidden in heavenly places. I am, however, going to show you how to deal with evil as it ties the two together in your life and surroundings. It is obvious that Satan did know that if he could get the first man to believe his lie about why God didn't want him to know something spiritually, mankind would lose his grip on every natural thing over which God had given him control. Furthermore, Satan knew that it would force everyone else to fight the new negative spiritual momentum that Adam could set in motion as father of the human race.

"But the Lord God warned him, 'You may freely eat the fruit of every tree in the garden-except the tree of the knowledge of good and evil. If you eat its fruit, you are sure to die'."
Genesis 23:16-17 NLT

The bad news is that we are all to blame. All of us are like the rest of us. Eve was the mother of us all and like her, we have all desired to know about good outside of its connection to God even though, like her, we weren't created when He gave the original command (notice she was created in verse 22 of the above passage). God knew what it would do to not only us, but all of creation and warned us but we chose Satan's insights instead. Because it took an act of disobedience to make that choice, God's resulting curse on everyone that walks on planet earth has produced a sinful tendency in all of us toward good's dark counterpart and enslaved us to the being, Satan, that models the behavior of disobedience. As a result, every person who has ever been born on this planet has gone through the same hopeless cycle of searching for a 'why' to the bad realities that he struggles to know what to do about in and around him.

"Then the Lord God said to the serpent, 'Because you have done this, you are cursed more than all animals, domestic and wild. You will crawl on your belly, groveling in the dust as long as you live. And I will cause hostility between you and the woman, and between your offspring and her offspring. He will strike your head, and you will strike his heel.' Then he said to the woman, 'I will sharpen the pain of your pregnancy, and in pain you will give birth. And you will desire to control your husband, but he will rule over you.' And to the man he said,

21

'Since you listened to your wife and ate from the tree whose fruit I commanded you not to eat, the ground is cursed because of you. All your life you will struggle to scratch a living from it. It will grow thorns and thistles for you, though you will eat of its grains. By the sweat of your brow will you have food to eat until you return to the ground from which you were made. For you were made from dust and to dust you will return'...Then the Lord God said, 'Look, the human beings have become like us, knowing both good and evil. What if they reach out, take fruit from the tree of life, and eat it? Then they will live forever!' So the lord God banished them from the Garden of Eden, and sent Adam out to cultivate the ground from which he had been made." **Genesis 3:14-19, 22-23 NLT**

The history of mankind is a history of loss. We lost the kingdom that our heavenly Father gave us and something inside all of us wants to get back to where we once belonged. *Eden* means pleasure and delight in Hebrew. Adam lost the ability to govern the entire earth from a real utopian position. What did he fail to do? The same thing we often fail to do today. We don't cultivate and guard our boundaries (Genesis 2:15) from the evil within. Humans once had all the power of beings created in God's own image, to rule natural things from a supernatural perspective with limitless ability. Imagine how successful Adam was with God's lavish generosity meeting him at every turn and the crowning gift of a perfect wife as his final blessing. This was no accidental small time fall from grace. In fact, it eerily paralleled Satan's fall, who ultimately engineered it. The fact that Adam lost it all so easily tells us that he must have had an incredible capacity to deal with dangers, both spiritual and natural.

The devil once fell from the highest places of spiritual reality himself. He likes us to either see ourselves as nothing, or think that we are 'all that', until it is too late to reverse our course. Why? Because he knows exactly what it feels like. The truth is that we have always been far more able to handle multi-dimensional things than we take the time to think about today. The lesson we need to learn is that we have to stay far more dependent on God than we usually want to take the responsibility for.

As bad as the bad news is, the even better 'good news' is that God's higher laws of motion are greater than "equal and opposite." Satan's actions, once carried out through earth's original parents, produced the reaction he was looking for; most of this reaction is still reverberating through the population to this day. Newtown, Connecticut, and many other cities prove that, if anything, the sheer wickedness of common crime is once again on the rise. However, the God of the Bible (YHWH) is the One who is making all things new (Revelation 21:5) and as such, specializes in making the current better.

Now that you know that these laws of motion matter to more than just the scientists among us, the predictable result of being ejected from Eden was a 'head smashing.' Sooner or later, a more than equal and opposite force for sin was going to emerge from God's own Word in that garden (Genesis 3:14), which would restore mankind's ability to be restored to God's original intention.

The great thing about God is that, of course, He had a better plan all along. He promised to restore all things by sending his Servant to right every wrong, declare new things and buy back everyone He has called (Isaiah 42-43). It's hard not to notice that only one person in history has enjoyed this level of complete mastery over creation with all its injustice and evil. Jesus Christ was opposite in many ways to Satan, but not equal by any measure. When He entered the human equation, He was what God's people had been looking for for 4,000 years, the answer to every 'why' that Satan had ever put in their heads. Born into a Roman world just as it was charting the course of modern history, Jesus spoke and acted in ways no man ever had before.

"When the Temple guards returned without having arrested Jesus, the leading priests and Pharisees demanded, 'Why didn't you bring him in?' 'We have never heard anyone speak

like this!' the guards responded. " John 7:45-46 NLT

"The disciples were amazed. 'Who is this man?' they asked. 'Even the winds and waves obey him!" Matthew 8:27 NLT

"When Jesus had finished saying these things, the crowds were amazed at his teaching, for he taught with real authority—quite unlike their teachers of religious law." Matthew 7:28-29 NLT

"Amazed, the people exclaimed, 'What authority and power this man's words possess! Even evil spirits obey him, and they flee at his command!" Luke 4:36 NLT

His 'gospel' (Greek for "good news") message was that of God's Kingdom being restored on this plane of existence once again. By giving His life, He transferred God's incredible power, like an unstoppable spiritual Newton's Cradle, back into motion among men. It has been perpetually banging out decision after decision after decision for God ever since, to an extent that has never been equaled in human history. Even as Satan's lie continued to work death in others, and even as He was opposed by those with suspicious motives on every side, evil was automatically stymied wherever Jesus went. This was because, through Him, God reversed the playing field by reintroducing the Tree of Life that man was originally intended to eat of and live forever, back into the human equation.

Check the New Testament for yourself and you will find references to the 'Kingdom of God' or the 'Kingdom of Heaven' over 100 times. Most of these come straight from the mouth of Jesus himself, connecting His mission to Daniel's promise of a coming "Son of Man" who would come carrying God's eternal dominion, glory and kingdom. The ultimate purpose? To raise up a people to possess this kingdom, eventually overwhelming every evil kingdom in the history of humanity (Daniel 7:13-27).

Jesus demonstrated the authority of heaven, and taught over forty parables to explain how it will overcome in the end plus how it works for those who will believe in Him now. Satan recognized Him so clearly and took His threat to the dominion that He had leveraged in this world so seriously, that he tempted Jesus personally, as he had Adam in the Garden of Eden in the beginning. However, God's own human death was the mysterious death-blow for the kingdom of darkness. Instead of working for Satan, it worked completely against him. Before he understood what was happening, God's apple had dropped, the world was watching and, try hard though he did, there was nothing the devil could do. The very people he had deceived into sinfully and wickedly killing the Lord of life, did just as God predicted they would, releasing the Old Testament prophetic words to further heaven's plan instead.

The worst part of it all for Satan is that it just keeps going. Wherever the message of the cross was told thereafter and wherever Jesus' name is genuinely and constantly praised today, God's power continues to transfer the same momentum through those who believe according to the power of that original resurrection force, by which the Holy Spirit restored Jesus' life! Now people everywhere have a choice. Wherever a person's heart turns to God, His power blasts out a new outlet for His dominion and glory, restoring the reality of Heaven's kingdom around others.

Evil does not completely cease to exist or suddenly leave even when people get serious about their faith. It is evident, however, that calamity did not follow Jesus around in the four Gospels, which chronicle His life and ministry. Deliverance and rescue followed Jesus. His disciples had the exact same power at work in them, which is why, through great struggle, they turned the Roman world up-side-down in a mere generation and took it over completely, in only a little over 300 years. It wasn't until Christianity became content to merely rule on a worldly, religious level, that darkness impeded its progress again. Satan's dark kingdom of evil no longer works anywhere that people know how to resist temptation, stop lies, reverse the effects of sin, and release heaven's light in Jesus' name. Physical laws of motion are working all around us right now whether we remember how they work or not. When we disregard and oppose them, we pay a price for our ignorance. It is even more true where spiritual law is concerned.

If we will start looking for God's apple in our current events, we are going to find truths that can relieve a lot of frustration today and save more people tomorrow. Take a closer look at the world just since the turn of the millennium. It isn't hard to see that evil is on the rise, but what about our willingness to do something about it? Anyone can choose to oppose evil and true Christians are key to reversing the prevailing conditions in their cities, regions, and countries because Jesus directly authorized them to use His spiritual force. Saints are not only the answer to sinners' legitimate questions about the goodness of God, their lives should be demonstrations of the power His Holy Spirit possesses to overcome even the most satanic forms of evil.

CHAPTER THREE
Our 1st Move

WE HAVEN'T BEEN THIS WAY BEFORE

My wife and I were returning from the Hartford airport early one morning in late 2011. We had just been delivering a group of guest ministers to their departing flight out of Connecticut. Our usual way home takes us through the wooded hills and valleys of the surrounding countryside with many twists and turns. Not having lived in Connecticut very long at the time, I unknowingly took a left where I should have taken a right, and ended up with a story to tell.

Because there were so many people, we had taken two vehicles which meant I was leading the way with my wife, Bobbi, following closely behind. I knew something was wrong as we drove through the village of Canton, but never having been this way before, coupled with the recent snowfall covering everything, I began to second guess my own memory about the road we were on. I thought that maybe I had just overlooked this short stretch of unfamiliar highway, but as we continued to drive, things seemed increasingly wrong about that last, left turn.

Heading back out into more open countryside, I finally decided things were definitely not right, so I signaled for Bobbi to turn into an empty parking lot. Pulling up beside her, I noticed a puzzled look across her face as she leaned out of her window holding her mobile phone. Looking back I am sure I just thought it, but I could have sworn I heard her say something like, "Where the hell are we?"

At first, I thought the frustration of following me had just gotten the best of her early morning emotions. Then I wondered if maybe the frustration of following a guy like me for so many years had simply come full circle in these last five miles of confusion. I finally decided it was probably the frustration that comes with a lifetime of ministry, which can sometimes push words that curse out of even the mouths of those God called to bless. That's when I snapped back into focus and read what was written in bold letters on the screen of her mobile GPS application.

As funny as it seemed later, we weren't necessarily smiling at the time. For reasons beyond the frustration of getting lost, nothing could have prepared me for what I saw. *Satan's Kingdom* is what the screen displayed. In fact, that's all it displayed, with no other words of explanation whatsoever. Bobbi hadn't been swearing at me after all, she was simply asking where we were in regard to what was now freaking us both out. It wasn't that it didn't make sense to us, it was that it made *too much* sense. Finding yourself in situations like this, does not necessarily mean that you are crazy. But sometimes they can be indicative of the crazy times we're all living in. They demand that we step back and look at the bigger picture. Let me explain.

Know Where You're Coming From

You have to understand where Bobbi and I come from. Bobbi knew very well that we have had demonic episodes in regard to technology, in the past. Experience has taught us that confronting problem situations is kind of what we do in the ministry. That can mean encounters with things not so normal. One particular church we pastored had so many unexplained problems when we arrived, that it was not uncommon for our office computers to shut down regularly for no apparent reason. I am not kidding—we had a haunted church. Once, while trying out a new dictation device, I was simply recording my opening greeting from a sermon and it was translated into text about the beast and the dragon straight from the Biblical book of Revelation. It was the first time I used this particular technology, so I was a novice, but there wasn't even a mention of that portion of scripture anywhere in the entire sermon. What was I dealing with that didn't want me to dictate the rest of that message? In the audio segment, I was simply saying hi, but so was someone else.

I realize that in America, we no longer think in terms of real spiritual dark entities, but oh how we love to create them for our movies, television programs, and video games. Halloween is big business because it allows our children to play around with the demonic without consciously admitting its full reality, even to ourselves, _the parents_. Connecticut itself is famous for some of its haunting stories and places. When you get more serious about following Jesus however, and start saying the words that He said with some heartfelt meaning, His enemies will get serious about showing up to block your path. Don't believe me? I dare you to try it.

"...as they try to keep us from preaching the Good News of salvation...We wanted very much to come to you, and I, Paul, tried again and again, but Satan prevented us." 1 Thessalonians 2:16-18 NLT

Back to Satan's Kingdom. Our journey to this puzzling destination in Connecticut turned out to be like a lot of trips people take through life all around this world. We weren't really in the devil's territory, but then again we really were. After looking around I noticed a snow covered sign across the road from where we had stopped, which upon closer inspection, marked the location of a state park with that exact name: Satan's Kingdom. Not that this was so much easier to wrap our heads around, but it did at least give me a reasonable explanation for the information on my wife's mobile phone. That was more than I have been able to say about the dictation device to this day.

So, Satan's Kingdom really is a park in the state I live in, I just didn't realize it at first because it was covered up. Satan's kingdom is also a real spiritual jurisdiction, located all around planet earth. Trust me, it is there. You just may not be able to see it yet because the signs you are passing on your way through life, have been covered up by circumstances around you. If you pay closer attention though, your circumstances will alert you every so often to things outside the ordinary, genuinely going on beyond the scope of your perception. Newtown's Law is one of those things. Similar to Newton's Law, it tells us to stop and look into the reasons for strange goings-on of a more spiritual nature around us. This will also challenge our sense of direction and at first, may be quite counterintuitive.

Newtown's Law says, "What happened to children in our town is not normal. It's not right and something more is going on than has met my eye." It leads us to look around and ask what dictates the motion of such events, and what are we not aware of, that may warn us of them sooner next time. Newtown's Law alerts us to the source of lawlessness by reminding us that Satan's kingdom has been at work in worldly events long before we noticed, or were willing to confront our lost condition. It uncovers the sign posts on our road to God's destination and teaches us where the trouble spots lie.

According to a mix of New England history and folklore, the state park that I happened onto derived its name from being a rough area of mountainous terrain in the earliest days of the nearby settlement of New Hartford. The natural landscape by nature, kept its citizens somewhat segregated from the rest of the town. Because of this unmarked boundary and who knows what else, some locals began referring to it as Satan's Kingdom. Some of these people were probably biased; others adhered to silly religious superstitions. However, there also may have been some dark realities associated with the area's people or past, which had crept into its present, like those curses that our Bibles speak of that do not come without cause.

Like many such things in life, the area eventually lived up to its name, becoming home to many transient outcast types who, after settling there, developed a reputation for the criminal element among their population. Over time, demographics changed, but the name remained. Today, strangely enough, it is a popular tranquil setting for outdoor enthusiasts. It is at least bizarre that we can get comfortable enough naturally, to live with such a spiritually uncomfortable name.

After the whole experience, I was just glad that I got lost in the new millennium and not the 18th or 19th centuries. I could turn around and find my way home, taking wife and wallet with me. The deeper spiritual lesson made its impression, however. It caused me to remember again how fine the line really is between physical and spiritual realms, and how easy it is to forget about it, when everything around us is moving along normally. In the end, taking a wrong turn wasn't the worst thing that could have happened that morning. Bobbi and I could have had an uneventful trip home and gone ahead with our lives as usual. Instead, we got both a good laugh and healthy reminder of how serious things in our neck of the woods really are.

Where are you coming from in life? It has everything to do with getting your bearings in regard to where you are going. What do you know about your own history and tendencies? Where has your town been in the past, and what are the prevailing cultural tendencies there today? The biggest weapon Satan has, is the darkness and deception he is partial to hiding himself in. He also prefers for you not to know. And what he likes better is your not wanting to know, because your own perception is skewed. According to the Bible, the whole world is lost in Satan's Kingdom today. I'm trying to get you to pull over and find out where you are.

If you don't think this includes the Christian world, ask yourself when you last heard a preacher at church or on television use the following scripture in his or her sermon:

"Now the Holy Spirit tells us clearly that in the last times some will turn away from the true faith; they will follow deceptive spirits and teachings that come from demons...Give your complete attention to these matters. Throw yourself into your tasks so that everyone will see your progress. Keep a close watch on how you live and on your teaching. Stay true to what is right for the sake of your own salvation and the salvation of those who hear you." 1 Timothy 2:1, 15-16 NLT

You Gotta Wanna Know

The truth is that Satan is happy to have a state park named after him, even if it is a bit strange at first glance. Satan wants no one to talk or think about him as a possible threat in real life. It works as a perfect cover for the unthinkable truth that He is there. He is happier when the name of the Lord is so overused that people begin subconsciously equating spirituality in general with myth, tradition, or even alternative forms of higher-conscious awareness. Skewing the lines of truth and error is what he is all about. He is counting on our human history of preferring not to worry too much about it. We reserve the right to assume there is no real harm in having parks with a hellish name, churches with only social values, and towns that are not concerned about either. The proverbial cracks are starting to show on the thin layer of ice that we are treading.

On my way back from the airport that morning I knew I was in the state of Connecticut, I just had no idea that there was an alternative state of reality along the road that I was traveling. This is a perfect picture of the two spiritual roads which diverge in the wood of life. God's kingdom and Satan's kingdom both exist in our world, along our paths, like it or not, and we are responsible to figure out where we are in reference to them at all times. They are the back story to many of the headlines we read and watch. But why wait to be surprised by the resulting circumstances of the wrong turns we have not realized we have made? Time itself will make sure we pull over for directions sooner or later, ready or not. It is best to recognize what is behind the scenes of our lives, ahead of time. This is what keeps all the demanding 'whys' answered before trouble comes. Without realizing it, we let the wrong kingdom create actions which demand that we spend all our time reacting.

If you wait to react, you're too late. Jesus called us into action by teaching us to pray to our Father in Heaven, in His name, initiating the coming of His kingdom and the materializing of His will. We are actually called to change the playing field by following God's own example. Jesus was the God-Human hybrid, who alone could pay the price to forgive our sins by dying and empower us to overcome evil by rising to life again. The antichrist will be the best attempt by the dark side, to reproduce those eternal results.

I probably don't need to remind you that the Bible says the antichrist will come up short. So, which team are you on? Which results are you looking for in your town? What is your church doing about it while occupying that space of ground that Jesus commissioned believers to fight for? Maybe you are just now realizing that you have been drafted by the wrong team. It's not too late to appeal to Jesus personally for an eternal transfer (reread the 'Caution' section at the beginning of this book right now).

The religious and political establishments of Jesus' day were reactionary like America is becoming. They wanted to know where He was coming from in His life and ministry, so He gave them interesting responses designed to get their attention. When His ambitious contemporaries in church leadership accused Him of false spirituality, He replied:

"Any Kingdom divided by civil war is doomed. A town or family splintered by feuding will fall apart. And if Satan is casting out Satan, he is divided and fighting against himself. His own kingdom will not survive...But if I am casting out demons by the Spirit of God, then the Kingdom of God has arrived among you. For who is powerful enough to enter the house of a strong man like Satan and plunder his goods? Only someone even stronger - someone who could tie him up and then plunder his house." **Matthew 12:25-26, 28-29 NLT**

To Jesus' political authorities, He made it clear that His fight was a real one that would first be fought on a spiritual plane with weapons which were not physical.

"My kingdom is not an earthly kingdom. If it were, my followers would fight...But my kingdom is not of this world...'You say I am a king. Actually, I was born and came into the world to testify to the truth. All who love the truth

recognize that what I say is true.' 'What is truth?' Pilate asked. Then he went out again to the people and told them, 'He is not guilty of any crime.'" **John 18:36-38 NLT**

People must stop periodically and verify which way they are headed. Much like my wife and me in this story, it can be helpful to do so sooner rather than later. The initial shock of finding out that you are not only lost but that you have ended up in the devil's territory, is more than many people today think they can turnaround from. The pressure of finding out you really are way outside of your comfort zone may be more than a little upsetting, but the reward of correcting your course is well worth it in the end. The Lord will help you. Just remember to open your heart and ask Him.

The Space between Good and Evil

Individuals, couples, churches, businesses, towns, regions and nations can adjust their headings on various levels. The circumstances of our time are presently demanding that adjustments be made. The temptation is to, once again, settle for politically driven ideological changes, which increasingly edge mankind ever closer to the brink of a final godless world order, foretold in scripture. Neither the religious, nor political establishments of Jesus' time, saw the working of God's or Satan's kingdom behind the events of their day, and few are willing to look close enough to see those same spiritual gaps which exist today. We can, however, decide to act in the authority and responsibility that God has given His followers. We can step into that space between where we are and where we are headed, with a prayerful mindset to think the thoughts of the Holy Spirit, like those original Christians who wrote the Bible did. The more we want to know, the quicker we may be able to reverse the momentum in our families, churches and cities.

What we learn from all of this is that spiritual motion is divided into two basic directions, toward God and away from Him. We understand the need to stop and clear our heads naturally in an empty parking lot somewhere when we are lost, but we don't understand this principle spiritually. Biblically speaking, it is evident how important these spaces between good and evil are to God. Not just individuals, but whole cities and nations are viewed in scripture as moving closer to His blessing or further into the danger zone of His judgment. Babylon, Nineveh, Sodom, Jericho, Tyre, Jerusalem, Israel and Egypt are all examples of places that were blessed, cursed or, at different times, both.

It is also interesting that God's judgment is individual by location depending on the specifics of each place. He is righteous and therefore cannot be unrighteous in His dealings, slow to anger, and full of tender mercies. The difference in their outcomes at various times, is how they handled the gaps or spaces afforded them with regard to measuring their circumstances by the things God had revealed to them. In the case of Sodom, Abraham was able to stand in the space between good and evil, between God and Sodom's citizens' unbridled sinfulness, to find what terms existed under which God would reverse the coming judgment. God agreed to save the whole city from the destruction it was bringing on itself if only ten righteous people could be found within its borders. (Genesis 18)

Where ancient Nineveh was concerned, the whole city repented at the initial preaching of one prophet and all were completely saved. People today are so touchy and anti-judgmental that they resist the notion, outright, that God is both good and punishing. Because of the existence of evil, He would be unrighteous if He acted any other way. Truthfully, who can fathom the depth of either His love or His willingness to save the most people possible, in any given situation? Contrarily, the devil's entire scheme is based upon exactly the opposite approach. He always seeks to trick humanity into opposing God's express directives knowing that the eventual result of believers own disobedience is the wrath of God. (Jonah 1-4; Romans 1:16-18))

God sent His own son, 2,000 years ago, as the only divinely

appointed hybrid-human-being ever created, a God-Man. His mercy is amazingly patient. If there ever were a cosmic crime worthy of total destruction, it would be to reject the man God became. God purposefully created a way of escape for all of us in Jesus Christ. The message this heavenly man carried, prevents God from fully judging sin until the fullness of time is fulfilled. He has set an incredibly long space of years between Calvary and that future date, proving that our very best outcome is His intention. Today, movie makers throw around the concept of hybrid humanism, exploring both the biological and technological possibilities of building a 'better man'. No need to get all sci-fi when God already did it and is simply waiting for everyone to receive the opportunity to recognize it.

What is needed, are believers getting in the middle of all this madness like modern Abrahams, stepping into the gaps that exist between God and man. Jesus is the great mediator and we, as His own extended body, are scripturally able to extend that same redemptive power and authority, to people and places, through the open door we have into the heavens. Therefore, when it comes to our own cities and towns, we have a tremendous responsibility to help release a grace (or godly ability) within and around them through prayer. Like Jonah, it is even possible to reverse at times, the outcome of a city or town with completely wicked tendencies. I think the biggest question we should ask in a place like Newtown, is not what did the people there do to incur such judgment, but rather what are Christians in towns everywhere willing to do today to protect their own populations?

My intention is not to assign blame for natural events but to point out ways we can address root sources. The first way to devil-proof our environment, is to expose that this cosmic personality is the problem. This allows us to move toward God's solution. Those who know the Lord have been given His eyes, ears, hands, feet, mind and Spirit, with which to save people, just like Jesus did. When confronted with evil, whether in general or in person, He used His God-given heavenly authority to resist, push back, and defeat it anywhere that it crossed paths with His divine assignment and destiny. He was the space between and so are we, in His place.

Nobody could have known that 28 people, mostly children, were going to violently lose their lives in our town, unless God Himself had told them. The problem, more often than we may like to imagine, is that believers, who have this ability to keep the space between heaven and earth open, can themselves become an issue. Remember Jonah? He was eaten by a huge fish because he did not want to go to Nineveh. Why? Because he knew there was a distinct possibility that, if they repented, God would forgive them. He actually wanted the city and all the people in it to die out of his own religious over-zealousness and cultural bias/prejudice. Biblically speaking, especially when Christians are more cohesively integrated with other believers, they are empowered to release people from the mindsets that Satan seeks to entrench in people and their societies.

How about Lot's wife? Scripture explicitly uses her as an example of someone who was being rescued by the mercy of God through Abraham's prayers, yet fell under His judgment in the process (Genesis 19:26). We have to know that the lack of belief in believers, can become the greatest of hindrances to both self and city. It's hard to forget a famous Christian couple in the most powerful early days of church history: Ananias and Sapphira. They were normal believers with an abnormal legacy. It is healthy for us to remember their demise. They were faithful, New Testament church goers killed by God—something rare under the mercy of Jesus' new covenant. What was their problem? It was simply that they treated their own sins as negligible in the context of a powerful move of the Holy Spirit blowing through their city (Acts 5:1-12). Again, God valued the souls of the many, over the selfish interests of the few who had lost His perspective in the process of distributing heaven's blessing across the community that they lived in.

Beyond what Christians seem to never be doing in towns across America where school shootings occur, there is always a secondary problem. What kind of things are going on there, secularly, that may not be pleasing to God or are directly connected to His chief enemy? We can't live like hell and then be shocked when some of it manifests in our surroundings. I mean, we *can*, but it won't make us a judgment-free zone—only the blood of Jesus can do that. It's always better in life to take an honest look at ourselves and the situations we get into. The best way to get out of something is to know how you got into it.

CHAPTER FOUR
Our 2ⁿᵈ Move

HEAD GAMES

The famous author of <u>The Hunger Games</u> trilogy resides in Newtown. Wouldn't you guess, she lives right in Sandy Hook? I am certainly not trying to infer that this person is in any way responsible for the violence that happened in the elementary school around the corner. Personally, I love the stories as a futuristic work of science fiction, but isn't it more than a little coincidental that they portray young children being violently killed in similar numbers to the real children here? So much of science is fiction, but then sometimes it seems like something else is working in the background—again—just beyond the boundary of what most towns today are willing to discuss.

Then there was that violent hurricane Sandy, which unpredictably turned left near a point also named Sandy Hook in New Jersey, just over a month before. That's not strange, until you realize it is. What about the supposed map depicting a similar area to Sandy Hook in a Batman movie? A Masonic Lodge in Sandy Hook named after Hiram, could be seen as spiritually suspicious when you know the not-so-secret identities of the two Hirams in scripture. One is the King of Tyre, noted by the prophet Isaiah as a covert, high-level, wicked spirit working through an earthly prince, for the purposes of the kingdom of darkness (Ezekiel 28:11-19). The other is a master craftsman sent to work for King Solomon from this same location. You'll probably remember that Solomon rose to the highest heights of God's goodness before falling to the lowest levels of evil but I'm sure it is just coincidence.

How about guys like me and all the other churches around town...what were we doing or not doing spiritually to promote the protection of God before such a thing transpired on our watch? The speculations are endless and I've heard all of the theories about what happened in Newtown and why. The same with Columbine before. There always seem to be strange anomalies, and we certainly should hold ourselves accountable. But only one thing is for sure: someone is killing our kids today on an unacceptable scale. I read somewhere that since 1999, in America alone, there have been over 90 school shootings incidences, when you include all the near misses! Instead of over-speculating, however, why don't we all just take a little spiritual responsibility for putting the finger on who Gods word says is ultimately responsible? From there we can work effectively to ensure we stop this insanity.

In a culture increasingly divided into those who want to either politicize or sensationalize everything I say we get serious about figuring out how God wants us to protect our own kids and exactly who we all need protection from. Policies are necessary but obviously limited in dealing with spiritual realities. Conspiracy theories are interesting but they don't usually lead anywhere worth going unless you are willing to go all the way. The Bible leads us directly to the one big, very real, cosmic conspiracy that God points out time and time again.

"A final word: Be strong in the Lord and in his mighty power. Put on all of God's armor so that you will be able to stand firm against all strategies of the devil. For we are not fighting against flesh-and-blood enemies, but against evil rulers and authorities of the unseen world, against mighty powers in this dark world, and against evil spirits in the heavenly places." **Ephesians 6:10-12 NLT**

The very word conspiracy tells us that there are true hidden plans and agendas in life but scripture always narrows them down to one specific source. The devil is the nasty, egotistical culprit capable of and actually orchestrating the most heinous of crimes. He is the psychopath responsible and the target that we must aim at without all the other distracting drama. The good news is that God is the master of coincidences and it just so happens that He has already done something to stifle every move Satan makes. You will notice how He always seems to have someone waiting in the wings in answer to every demon conspiring against His plans. Therefore, fear is not necessary for a blood-bought saint. Jesus has given believers the power of attorney in His own name, to rule over all the power of this enemy, but we are also commanded to keep our eyes on him at all times so as not to be fooled by his inevitable schemes (Luke 10:19; 2 Corinthians 2:11).

The Way Devils Play

The words *Satan* and *devil* have specific, respective meanings. Get a Bible dictionary or concordance and you will find out how the dark side operates through the definitions that God uses for this fallen angel. *Satan* is of Chaldean origin, which means it goes all the way back to that bastion of spiritual rebellion and arrogance, Babylon. It means *the accuser. Devil,* on the other hand, means *traducer or one who misrepresents, speaks ill of, or disparages.* Taken together, we can learn a valuable lesson. God's enemy is a blamer and a head games expert, who loves to start a fight but slip away before the cops come. Then, whoever goes to jail, sits in his or her cell wondering what happened and why.

There are other Biblical descriptions of the devil. Knowing them can help us devil-proof our lives, families, and cities. Jesus defeated Satan at the same game that Adam lost in the garden, because He knew a few important spiritual things: He knew Who God was, He knew who Satan was, and He knew what ground He needed to stand on. After three questions, Satan fled the wilderness that he had tried to trap Jesus in (Luke 4). The result? Jesus went back to town, full of God and His power, to set other captives free.

Adversary is used in 1Peter 5:8, describing the devil as an opponent in a lawsuit. Again he doesn't have unlimited power to destroy people's lives. He has to turn you against God or good, to obtain the right to inflict evil on this planet. Our job is to be sober and vigilant in our resistance. As I write this, our kids are gearing up for Halloween. Most will say that there is nothing wrong with hanging the devil all over town (along with other creepy spiritual entities), but it's one of those things that we do for fun, eerily beyond the boundaries that God sets for dealing with the devil. I understand people celebrate Halloween in towns all over the world, and violence does not erupt in their towns as a direct result…but what if in some towns, it does?

This scripture goes on to further describe the devil as a roaring lion, arrogantly trying to intimidate those within his destructive grasp. 1 Thessalonians 3:5 refers to Satan as the tempter, scrutinizing people and testing their susceptibility to his enticements. He is the deceiver mentioned in 2 Corinthians 11:3, seeking to completely seduce sinner and saint alike. Only a few sentences further down that same page, Satan is called a transformer, who disguises himself as an angel of light when the situation suits. If he can't stop you that way, he will hinder your path with tedious attention to detail, so as to impede your progress and wound your soul (1 Thessalonians 2:18).

Ephesians 2:2 defines Satan as the "prince of the power of the air." This tells us that he operates from the heavenly dimension, just above our natural surroundings, as the highest of a network of fallen beings, holding supernatural influence over the inhabitants of planet earth. 2 Corinthians 4:4 goes a step further, literally calling him the god of this age, the chief ruling magistrate of the system he set up through his evil genius to run this world by. Finally, Satan is the thief that Jesus called out in John 10:10, bent on taking everything God has given to us.

The devil is a formidable foe. We must know this enemy keeps a close enough watch on us to stay prepared, which is why we need to stay alert for signs of him at all times. Don't let me give you the superstitious impression that the devil is stronger than he is, or that he can take us down on his own. Again, his strategy is to infiltrate our thoughts until we think we're doing all the thinking. He never goes to jail for his crime, the people he instigates trouble for, do. He is an expert at using 'us against us' so we will feel all the shame, pay the highest price, and take all of the blame. Most importantly of all, He works to remove God's thoughts from people's thinking at all costs. He does not want you to learn the number one name for him in the Bible: Defeated.

"[But] he who commits sin [who practices evildoing] is of the devil [takes his character from the evil one], for the devil has sinned violated the divine law) from the beginning. The reason the Son of God was made manifest (visible) was to undo (destroy, loosen, and dissolve) the works the devil [has done]. 1 John 3:8 AMP**

Satan hates exposure to the light, just like all of those vampires in the movies that America loves. Wherever you find evil, you are going to find the devil hiding out in the background somewhere playing on people's emotions to keep things moving his way. Ever notice how vampires are so romantically appealing or Halloween is made to be so much fun? Satan does a good job of keeping people disarmed, knowing in reality that he is the bomb that has been disarmed. He needs you to think he is still ticking with all the same power he had before Jesus defeated him, in cosmic combat. Don't be fooled into thinking that there is nothing we can do to fight evil. The truth is, everything has been done about it and how you approach your surroundings with God's truth, can make all the difference.

"[God] disarmed the principalities and powers that were ranged against us and made a bold display and public example of them, in triumphing over them in him and in it [the cross]." Colossians 2:15 AMP

Along with Satan's names, there are plenty of ways, mentioned in scripture, that allow the devil to play head games with people. As a thieving seducer, he is seeking to steal God's word out of our minds before it has a chance to register on your heart (Matthew 13:19). He is looking to plant his own thoughts in our minds, corrupting our thinking until our mindsets are opposite to God's. He will beguile, belittle, blind, and batter us, until we are so weary that we only want to quit. His endgame is to steal what we have, kill who we are, and

47

destroy any good that we do. All of this taken together equals a working definition for evil. Like I said, it simply puts the "D" back in evil, when you expose this angel who fell like lightening from heaven for thinking he could be above the Most High God.

The problem with seduction is that the fall feels so good. Adam followed Satan and he fell into sin along with his wife and the whole human race. That opened a spiritual door and then hell had a way to break loose on earth. We have to not only understand the truth of our own deception in this, but we must also recognize that our feelings work to keep it that way. God has empowered us to enjoy another reality through the open door that is Jesus Christ. God Himself made a way to walk back into the light of the highest heaven, but it requires that we choose to believe against all the movement, momentum, and reactions of the world around us.

The Ark Will Always Lead You Out of Danger

Let me remind you of an important Old Testament story, which teaches us how to prepare for the battle between these two kingdoms. The opening chapters of Joshua tell us how God instructed him to lead the children of Israel up to the Jordan River in preparation for crossing over and attacking the Canaanite city of Jericho. It is an essay on how to walk with God and win our battles on many levels. In Joshua, an army was being trained in a warfare that would change natural circumstances by being fought first in the spirit realm. A leadership model was also being developed to maintain the Promised Land that God was giving His people. Both the army and the leadership were being taught how to take ground in the following years, by taking the first piece correctly.

In chapter three, we find Joshua giving the Lord's instructions for crossing the river in their initial approach to Jericho, just on the other side. Interestingly, the people at large were commanded to pay close attention to the priestly portion of their population, while advancing. These priests would be carrying the most important thing in the possession of the nation, the mysterious Ark of the

Covenant. (Think *Raiders of the Lost Ark* here for a minute to get the picture.) This piece of finely crafted furniture, held sacred items significant to the memory of the miraculous things that God had performed on their behalf since the time of their deliverance from Egypt. They are too numerous to recount here, but just remember what God did for these chosen people. That is one reason for this Ark, or treasure chest, of their spiritual heritage.

More importantly, the Ark literally represented the presence of God, Himself. It not only contained a supernatural ability to display His Holy Spirit, but it also served as a figure of the spiritual dwelling place that He was restoring in His relationship with fallen mankind. In so many ways, this lavish box was not only a present indicator of God's promise to be with them, but more importantly an eternal commitment on His part to send the One (Jesus the Messiah) that would house the fullness of the godhead in a Body. It then had to be everything to them—their primary focus and reminder that God was their sovereign leader, the One Who gave them the victory before the fight.

Today, on this side of the Cross, authentic Christians carry that fullness of Jesus transferred to them, especially when taken as a whole unit. In unified groups, we exert tremendous influence over all sources of evil.

"And [so that you can know and understand] what is the immeasurable and unlimited and surpassing greatness of His power in and for us who believe, as demonstrated in the working of His mighty strength, which He exerted in Christ when He raised Him from the dead and seated Him at His [own] right hand in the heavenly [places]," Far above all rule and authority and power and dominion and every name that is named [above every title that can be conferred], not only in this age and in this world, but also in the age and the world which are to come. And He has put all things under His feet and has appointed Him the universal and supreme Head of the church [a headship exercised throughout the church], [Ps.

49

8:6] Which is His body, the fullness of Him Who fills all in all [for in that body lives the full measure of Him Who makes everything complete, and Who fills everything everywhere with Himself]." **Ephesians 1:19-23 AMP**

How do we harness this truth in a practical way that can be used more effectively in today's world? The rest of this book will give us a few steps to take in the right direction. Before we take these steps, however, we must really stop to recognize what we are dealing with. First, we have an enemy with a kingdom, intent on taking what God has given us. Second, and most important, we have a God Who is the Real Deal, intent on saving us completely. He is so great that our attention is demanded in order to move with Him.

Finally Joshua, (who is an Old Testament type of Jesus, with the same basic Hebrew name, Y'howshua) gave specific instructions that the Ark was to go ahead of the Israelites. Notice it was to be given an exact amount of space to serve its function in.

"Yet a space must be kept between you and it, about 2,000 cubits by measure; come not near it, that you may [be able to see the Ark and] know the way you must go, for you have not passed this way before." **Joshua 3:4 AMP**

This measurement was somewhere between one-half and four-fifths of a mile (depending on whose calculations of the ancient cubit you use). Isaac Newton seemed to lean toward the latter in formulating his theories and calculations for the measurement of gravity, time and space. Out of his understanding, came the knowledge of the need to account for the arc of the earth when measuring all true distances across a circular planet. In short, God has bound us into a physical reality that He is bigger than the sum total of. The point is that we really need to take Him into account when navigating our way through this life on every level.

Joshua likely did not know everything Isaac Newton later discovered, but he and his followers had been learning the theory of following the movements of God, in a similar fashion, throughout their forty years wandering in the wilderness of disobedience. As a side note, God also directed Noah to build an ark by which to escape the greatest destruction of evil the world had ever known. I think He is trying to tell us something here. Remember, God knows all the equations, so we need to trust His lead. The children of Israel were not going to just barge into the Promised Land their own way that day. They were going to give God the space that He demanded and separate themselves unto His authority to control their situation. It's the overriding principle behind my thoughts in this book.

"And Joshua said to the people, Sanctify yourselves [that is, separate yourselves for a special holy purpose], for tomorrow the Lord will do wonders among you." Joshua 3:5 AMP

Once they did this, the miraculous victories just kept coming. God showed them how to cross the Jordan River on dry ground like their forefathers had crossed the Red Sea, a generation earlier. Next, they learned to follow God's instructions very carefully. As long as they followed Him His way, separating themselves to His intentions, the walls of that city would fall down. When they shouted after the 13th lap around what amounted to the spiritual doorway, blocking their possession of this pagan land, the walls fell down and they destroyed the city.

This was, at once, a blessing and a curse. God's chosen people, if they would continue choosing to walk with Him as Adam originally did in the Garden, would receive the land at the center of this world for their inheritance. The Canaanites who lived there were conversely losing this land in judgment for their centuries' old refusal to repent and serve the same God of their forefather, Noah. The land was so dark that giants still lived there openly among the population. Their very existence describes a level of wickedness and violence known in the days of Noah's flood. Thirteen laps by God's people, who possessed neither chariots nor horses for warfare, spelled doom for this advanced civilization of people, while simultaneously mapping out a new hope for Israel.

Doing God's Math

Think about the implications. God commanded the Israelites to walk around Jericho once a day, for six days. Six in scripture is the number of man. They were to encircle the city seven times on the seventh day. Seven is the number of God's perfection. The Lord was using them to paint a picture of redemption for the inhabitants of the land. Six days is a long time to think, just like 6,000 years has been for mankind as a whole, today. We can always choose to accept the situation that we find ourselves in and call on God's mercy to save us when chaos and confusion surround us.

Inside Jericho there was a harlot named Rahab, with a scarlet rope hanging out of her window, because she had already seen the bigger picture (Joshua 2 & 6:17-25). She and her entire family were saved because she chose to see what was really going on around her, and separate herself from the wickedness of her city by appealing to Joshua's advanced spies, and ultimately to the kindness of God.

"...for the Lord your God, He is God in heaven above, and in earth beneath." Joshua 2:11

His mercy is so great this very woman, a harlot, is found in the lineage of Jesus Christ Himself, along with some other ladies with foreign blood and/or ill repute (Ruth and Tamar, see Matthew 1:3-6). These six days represent God's love and patience with lost people. It represents a window of opportunity to embrace His redeeming nature before the 7th day of His reckoning arrives. He wants us to see truth and choose life while we still can.

The seven laps on the seventh day emphasize this principle and show us that there is a real spiritual clock keeping perfect time. God has organized all things. Jesus' entrance into time was the motion by which many otherwise sure judgments like this one are now postponed and often cancelled. Believers who act on knowing God, instead of what they have known about God, create real spiritual motion, generating a reaction in the spirit realm and changing things in this world. Only knowing about God is a trick of Satan, reengineering a type of Christianity in people's reality, that is only powerful on a natural plane (politically, socially, emotionally, traditionally, etc.). In other words, if someone doesn't really know God the way Joshua did, nobody else is going to end up marching around the walls of this world's Jerichos.

God was showing everyone, including the fallen spirit world, that it was time for the restoration of mankind to kick into gear. Seven days, just like in the beginning of creation, represent the perfection of His work. In a land where moon worship was the prevailing religion, seven times around Jericho, (which is translated as the 'city of the moon') spelled the beginning of a complete end for the kingdom of darkness. As the universe moves in circles of motion, God moves spiritually in a similar fashion, always connecting beginning to end. What played out in this Bible story was a spiritual battle, motion against motion, between the two kingdoms, for this key ground on the planet.

As I mentioned in an earlier chapter, the Bible says that God actually *is* the Beginning and the End (Revelation 1:8 & Genesis 1:1). It also says that Jesus, being the exact visible representation of the invisible God, existed before all things and in Him all things consist. By Him all things were created, existing through Him and for Him (Colossians 1:15-18). God exhibits a somewhat circular approach to time, wouldn't you say? He is the circle around our linear reality. Somehow He is *"...sustaining everything by the mighty power of his command."* **Hebrews 1:3 NLT**

Knowing this, the devil has tried to create a similar kind of motion around mankind as an alternative to God's motion. He is also a heavenly being whose operations are centered in the spiritual dimension. From there, he seeks to keep people's minds off the Ark, if you will. He needs us to be so preoccupied that we don't have time to give back to the God, who gave us all the time in the world. In this way the devil prevents us from crossing our Jordan's, surrounding our cities, and breaking down the walls he, himself has erected to prevent God from making sense. He will go to the greatest lengths at his disposal to do this, which is why we must learn God's ways again.

Today, we find ourselves in this same position, needing to hear these same words because God has also given us a divine inheritance. This time, the whole world is our ground and Jesus' Word is our weapon to finish the job spiritually, that the Israelites never did on this physical plane. To do so, we have to take these same words more seriously, *"...you have never traveled this way before."* **Joshua 3:4 NLT**

CHAPTER FIVE
Our 3rd Move

THE FIRST LAW OF SPIRITUAL MOTION:
THE LAW OF THE SPIRIT

We are now ready to outline the specific mechanics which make up what I call, the 'Spiritual Law of Motion' or 'Newtown's Law.' Jesus revolutionized how men move with God, being the fulfillment of every Old Testament promise and the model of a new, life-changing way of walking. Those who first followed Him were remarkable in their almost immediate ability to step into it. We find a New Testament principle, in the writings of these men, that is strikingly similar to the three-in-one formula which makes up what is often thought of as, Newton's singular Law of Motion. Over the next three chapters, I will describe each law and show how we can use them together to create momentum for good both in, and around our lives.

The 3 in 1 Law of Spiritual Motion

If you simply apply this information, I promise that you will begin to see the kinds of results that people in the Bible experienced when faced with evil. This is the best company in history to be in, when you run into bad situations. As we will see, spiritual motion in God is the key to overcoming the tendency toward evil in yourself, other people, and the places that we all live. It's not that we are going to stamp out all darkness and trouble, but by walking with the One who will and following God's lead, we can tap His ability to attack the root of crime. Here is the three-step spiritual law of motion:

"So be subject to God. Resist the devil [stand firm against him]. And he will flee from you." **James 4:7 NLT**

One simple Bible verse sounds a lot like Newton's Laws of Motion, set in religious language. We know from his own writings, Sir Isaac combed through scripture in his quest for answers to many of the scientific mysteries he sought to answer, so the similarity in thought isn't surprising. It was written in our Bibles however, long before Newton discovered how to apply it to mankind's understanding of physical properties. A few hundred years later, tragedies like the one in Newtown, are reminding us just how desperately we need to revisit scripture with this same attitude. The mysteries we are faced with today are pressing us to find answers as well.

"This most beautiful system of the sun, planets, and comets, could only proceed from the counsel and dominion of an intelligent and powerful Being....This Being governs all things, not as the soul of the world, but as Lord over all; and on account of his dominion he is wont to be called Lord God "pantokrator," or Universal Ruler...." **Isaac Newton**

As truly great as God is and as uniquely gifted as men like Isaac Newton were, the simplicity behind the complexities of life is what makes both, even greater. Nowhere is this more evident than in the Bible itself. When we search for truth in the Bible, we find more than reality. We find the way to grasp it and the life of the One it leads us to experience. The Lord keeps it simple for those with a heart toward Him. He 'devil-proofs our lives by keeping us first focused on Him rather than the wealth of information about Him which can make Him so interesting.

"But I fear, lest somehow, as the serpent deceived Eve by his craftiness, so your minds may be corrupted from the simplicity that is in Christ." **2 Corinthians 11:3 NKJV**

Early Christian leaders like James, the author of our earlier text (James 4:7), and Paul, the writer above (2 Corinthians 11:3), understood the two different concepts that I have been discussing in this book. They knew that there was and is a dark spiritual force with a face set against us, which absolutely needs to be resisted, both from within, because of our own sinful condition and without, because of the world's group-tendency toward sin. More importantly, they knew that the one force that was and is more powerful was the Lord God. The Bible clearly teaches that any person or group who will submit themselves to God, can repel the devil's advances of evil wherever they are encountered. So, the overarching law of spirituality is to first know God Himself, as these people did, and then begin to address our problems through His power.

Paul said it this way:

"Therefore, [there is] now no condemnation (no adjudging guilty of wrong) for those who are in Christ Jesus, who live [and] walk not after the dictates of the flesh, but after the dictates of the Spirit. [John 3:18.] For the law of the Spirit of life [which is] in Christ Jesus [the law of our new being] has freed me from the law of sin and of death. For God has done what the Law (of Moses) could not do, [its power] being weakened by the flesh [the entire nature of man without the Holy Spirit]. Sending His own Son in the guise of sinful flesh and as an offering for sin, [God] condemned sin in the flesh [subdued, overcame, deprived it of its power over all who accept that sacrifice], [Leviticus 7:37.] So that the righteous and just requirement of the Law might be fully met in us who live and move not in the ways of the flesh but in the ways of the Spirit..." **Romans 8:1-4 AMP**

Look closely and you will again see this three-in-one principle. It probably shows up in so many scriptures because God is the three-in-one Author. The Father addresses a situation, the Son steps forward to take action and the Holy Spirit ensures the results. We get to make a decision with the free will God gave us to either follow that lead or take our own path in life. Accepting Jesus as God's gift, cancels out the overpowering dictates of our fallen nature (which Satan so effectively uses against us) and leads us into the freedom of a new kind of life that only the Holy Spirit can breathe into the depths of our being. This is the Law of Spiritual Motion...it will always work to create positive or reverse negative momentum in our lives by applying God's force to the root of our issues.

Running to Win

Let's talk sports for a minute. Athletics can help define how motion works in a person's spiritual life to establish momentum on their home field. If you've ever had a major team from your region win the ultimate prize in its sport, you know how this win affects the atmosphere there, by generating a positive buzz in people. As I stated earlier, God has given all people the ultimate victory in advance, through the authority gained when Jesus Christ first addressed and then defeated the devil, once and for all. We have to believe it however, and use the spiritual momentum it has afforded us in the same way the Lord did, to maintain its life-changing effects in our everyday lives. The problem is that today many believers seem to have forgotten what Jesus Christ did for them, or worse, forgotten that His sacrifice was mandatory for their own, and others' peace and safety.

"...So run to win! All athletes are disciplined in their training. They do it to win a prize that will fade away, but we do it for an eternal prize. So I run with purpose in every step. I am not just shadowboxing." **1 Corinthians 9:24-26 NLT**

There are several references in the New Testament that compare sport to the way a Christian must walk, in order to make a difference. We have to compete with the reality of the spiritual situation that we are in on this planet, or we will lose the ground that God has given us to enjoy. Two sports, golf and boxing, will work for our purposes here. Golf wasn't invented at the time of the writing of the Bible, but you can see how the Bible uses boxing as a direct comparison to the fight of faith, with which, we win the spiritual battles Satan seeks to force us into. A boxer fights an opponent and a golfer plays against the whole field at once, but they both require precision movement to win.

Think about it with me. Boxing requires an opposing participant to put motion into action. For a fighter to be successful, he has to do the same three basic things that our scripture calls for when he steps into the ring. One, he has to answer the bell. Of course, it is easier to do this if he has already submitted to training, so he is ready for fight night, both physically and mentally. Second, a boxer has to keep his head in the match. He has to use his own force to intentionally resist his opponent. Third, he has to finish what he starts. A boxer has to stick to his game plan, for as long as it takes to wear his opponent down and get them to flee the ring in defeat.

I have my own story in regard to boxing. Entering the sixth grade, I was known as the toughest kid in my elementary school. This reputation was surprising to me since I had never fought one real fight up to that point in my life. What all the other kids thought about me was simply the result of my having a big mouth (even though I was one of the smallest guys in my class). Over time, I began to enjoy the perks of my unearned title. I believed what was being said about me, even though I had no action to back it up. It was good while it lasted, but the day came when I had to prove the title or lose it.

Another kid in my neighborhood knew that I wasn't as tough as everyone else in town thought I was. So, he decided to risk what little reputation he had in an effort to get what I had. We were both from the bad side of town, so from his point of view, he had nothing to lose and everything to gain. Maybe he thought if he beat me up, our classmates from the good side of town might give him the recognition they had instead offered me. The lesson I learned the day that he called me out, is the same one we're discussing here. I chose to fight back that day, but because inside I was untested and secretly afraid of losing, I didn't finish. When I panicked and ran home because I couldn't take the pressure of a crowd rooting against me for the first time in my life, it cost me more in the long run than if I had never had the reputation to start with.

As Christians, we do not have to wonder whether there is someone waiting to call us out, because Jesus has already exposed him. The question is, are we going to fight? Spiritually speaking, we are called to do so, not for reputation's sake, but to keep the bullies off our block. I learned a valuable lesson when I was twelve years old that has stuck with me for a lifetime: spend your energies moving toward being the real you and fighting for what counts, so you won't get caught pretending to be who everyone else thinks you are.

The laws of spiritual motion say that you have to fight for God's rights. Everybody knows that it is a crime to stand by and watch while someone else is being victimized. Yet, it is a common occurrence, because secretly people are afraid of getting hurt or losing something themselves. When it comes to stopping evil in society, people have to choose to move into the fight. The same criminal who takes your neighbor's goods will come for yours in due time, if you don't say no.

Par for Life's Course

I became a much better golfer when I owned a house on a golf course in Colorado, for several years. The thing that I learned there was, although golf is quite addicting, it is not quite the relaxing getaway that many make it out to be. In fact, I found it so similar to everyday life that I feel fortunate to have spent some time practicing its required skills. You can only get better by playing golf regularly, which means going over the same kinds of motions again and again. Unlike boxing, golf is not in the Bible, but it is a lot like reading the Bible. The more you read, the more you realize that you are being read.

The mechanics of golf also start with a foundation of knowing how to use motion to your advantage. When addressing the ball on the tee, a golfer must make the first move. When playing baseball or tennis, the ball is often propelled toward you first, awaiting your reaction. The golfer however, has to deal with Newton's 1st Law of Motion differently. *Inertia* is the term Newton used to point out that unless someone hits a ball that is not already in motion, it is not going anywhere. Simply put, you have to move to get the ball to move. Once you do, Newton's 2nd Law of Motion comes into play (literally), reminding you to regulate the force or speed with which you wish the mass (the golf ball) to accelerate at.

Because of the variables involved with regard to direction and distance, golf club manufacturers have given us many choices in selecting our equipment for different kinds of shots. This is largely due to Newton's 3rd Law, which tells us that all of our actions, both ahead of time and at present, will factor in to create a mirrored reaction. This third law is the law that everyone remembers, because it determines the outcome of motion, more than the other two. We can put a ball into play, but the precise way we come in contact with that ball is what really counts. Life mirrors this on many levels, but maybe none more clearly than the spiritual one.

In one way, golf, boxing, or even some aspects of everyday life would be so much easier if it weren't for gravity. We all know that gravity is the force around our planet, that keeps things grounded unless moved with force. It naturally produces something called friction, which becomes either our friend or foe, depending on the conditions and our considerations of said conditions. Friction factors into our golf game in every way. It determines whether we ever swing at a golf ball and if so, how much force we can exert to swing. Even after we've swung, friction still limits the golf ball's flight in nothing but open air.

We could hit golf balls amazingly farther and endure the fight much longer if there were no gravitational force to deal with, but there is. We don't usually complain about it, though. We have just become accustomed to it mentally and almost automatically compensate for it physically. Life's version of friction is seen in the bumper-sticker that says, *Stuff happens, Get Over It!* There are a couple of different versions of that sticker, but it has become a common saying because we all know the feeling. It is simply a description of the frustration we sometimes feel when 'playing' life.

Golf is a particularly interesting comparison to life for me. I am not the first one to make the connection, but maybe I can use it here to help us get ahead of the dangerous courses that we all face. Before we talk about the first Spiritual Law of Motion, it is important to stop and remember that like golf, everybody has a handicap (all of your accumulated scores over your golfing career, averaged out) to tell them where their motion in life has brought them thus far. We all face the same spiritual obstacles, just like we all face the same natural elements. How have we handled submission to God and resistance to the devil in the past? Have we followed Jesus and experienced freedom's victories, or is it just an opinion that we subscribe to?

In golf, our handicap takes into consideration how we have played and helps us determine how well we can play. Whether we have kept score on our cards or just in our heads, knowing that we can make good shots is what gives us the desire to make more. In other words, taking swings is what drives us to keep taking swings.

Not only did 'stuff' happen to us in the past, but it is happening all around us all the time. Winds are changing, moisture or lack of it is accumulating, people are playing in front of us while others push from behind. We lose balls, run out of tees, and get hotter or colder all within the duration of one round. This creates an even bigger demand for the right reactions on our part. The best golfers learn to go inside themselves when things around them are shifting. This blocks out the negatives and allows them to picture those positive moves they have executed so many times before.

This is what we have to do to engage the first law of spiritual motion. We must gather ourselves and regroup before taking that next swing. Stuff has happened, but now we realize that there is someone else behind those goings on. We cannot control every variable, but we can however, deal with ourselves. We know the rest of that equation. Stuff will keep on happening until and unless someone deals with it.

Tragedies like the one in Newtown, have proven that they will keep happening. They are fast becoming par for our cultural course. So who will gather themselves with the intention of getting to that inward place where the Kingdom of God can be observed, in preparation for taking a new swing (Luke 17:20-21)? Who is willing to use a different force to generate a new momentum and create a different outcome? This is what a counterpunching believer or a spiritual golfer has to do.

Another Law

There is an obvious negative side to life that some people have attributed to *Murphy's Law*, on account of its tendency to operate like a spiritual kind of gravity. This term is the recognition of a very real force that wants to pull everything down, even though deep inside we all want to rise up and thrive. In Paul's desire to be a good religious person and do right by God, he found a common roadblock. As much as He desired to live by God's written Law as established by his own Jewish heritage, he fell so far short that he sometimes despaired even of life. This struggle led him to compare his real life condition with the standard that God naturally set as a perfect spiritual being. Only after his encounter with Jesus on the road to Damascus (Acts 9:1-22), was Paul able to look back and discover the overcoming mechanics of our 1st Law of Spiritual Motion.

"I find therefore the law of my nature to be that when I desire to do what is right, evil is lying in ambush for me. For in my inmost self all my sympathy is with the Law of God; but I discover within me a different Law at war with the Law of my understanding, and leading me captive to the Law which is everywhere at work in my body—the Law of sin. (Unhappy man that I am! Who will rescue me from this death-burdened body? Thanks be to God THROUGH Jesus Christ our Lord!) to sum up then, with my understanding, I—my true self—am in servitude to the Law of God, but with my lower nature I am in servitude to the Law of sin." **Romans 7:21-25 WEY**

Paul actually identifies two opposing laws here, or hard-and-fast rules, which any person will encounter in life: God's way of doing things vs. the self-centered way of doing things without God. This is where it can get tricky for a religious person, but trust me, if you are spiritually minded, it is not that hard to wrap your head around the difference between God's ways and your own. God's people want to do things His way, but they encounter a friction that stops them from freely doing so. Even people who do not yet know God, usually have a pretty good idea that something in them is stopping them from making that first move. So, what we do about it is Jesus!

Paul's greatest discovery was the one he found through relationship with Jesus Christ when confronted with his handicap in life. There is a powerful force at work in God, that we must also find if we wish to overcome the discouraging human condition that we are all too familiar with. Paul realized he was dealing with the *Law of Sin* every time he tried in his own human ability to move forward with God. It is more powerful than the law governing natural life here on earth, because it is spiritual in nature, which is why the devil worked so hard to deceive Adam in the Garden. He knew by his own spiritual experience with *lawlessness,* what it would do to us if we only disobeyed one simple instruction while living in our original spiritually natural state.

The good news is that Jesus reversed its effects by demonstrating and then dying to transfer an opposite kind of momentum to humanity. He took upon Himself the humble position of becoming a man like us, so that we could learn how to step back into a spiritual condition from which to restore mankind's upward movement in God. He died to pay the penalty for all of our sin that works in and around us to keep us caught up in a battle of willpower that we cannot win alone. God gave us His own Son so that we could walk forward in life, from the position of that same restored relationship with Him that Paul found.

The 1ˢᵗ Law of Spiritual Motion

Remember our discussion on opposites in the first chapter and how they define each other? The laws of motion, whether natural or spiritual work just like that. We are either going forward or backward, up or down. Momentum is either working for or against us, we're either winning or losing. The first law of spiritual motion is the obvious opposite to our natural experience in life. Life is simply greater than death. The righteous quality of life displayed in Jesus Christ is much greater than the death which results from sin in this world. It IS the law that defines how God's power in us, raises us up into an overcoming experience.

"...Who will free me from this life that is dominated by sin and death? Thank God! The answer is in Jesus Christ our Lord. So you see how it is:...So now there is no condemnation for those who belong to Christ Jesus. And because you belong to him, the power of the life-giving Spirit has freed you from the power of sin that leads to death." **Romans 7:2 NLT**

'Knowing God' was the law of the Garden of Eden that Jesus restored. Spiritual freedom is a natural result of not only what Jesus has done for us, but who He is in and around us. Adam and Eve didn't know anything different until they chose sin and we can't know release from sin until we come back into relationship with the Lord. The 1ˢᵗ law of spiritual motion is the Law of the Spirit of Life that is resident in Christ Jesus. In order to engage its energy in our lives, we must walk in a maintained relationship with Him.

Go back to the golf illustration and identify what you are dealing with. Inertia exists for everyone who addresses the God equation, friction is just waiting for them to move. Both forces oppose anyone from hitting the ball that will bring them to God's 'green' again. The first law of Spiritual Momentum helps us to get past Murphy's Law by setting our thoughts on God's Spirit instead. From this tee box, we can make the kind of swings in life that will find His fairways and greens.

For example, the best golfers are those who can pay attention to the multiple details involved in golf, while remaining relaxed enough to play it as a game. Although it can be played in many different styles, the sport has to be approached from the standpoint of both concentration and relaxation, at the same time. Like life, it requires a certain kind of working knowledge—the kind that knows which actions to take in order to spark the reactions needed to cultivate winning momentum. Before his conversion, the apostle Paul was trying to serve God based on a set of rules and his good intentions. He discovered that sin easily kept that approach enslaved to its own directions. After conversion, Paul turns around like a master golf instructor and tells us the secret is simply letting the God of motion, play through us!

Know Your Handicap

Needless to say that not everybody can play golf and, of all those who can, not all of them can be considered good. Achieving par on any golf course, even an easy one is far from average. To break even in this game, you have to be better than most. Life seems similar to me in that if you want to make the most of it, you can't get by on intellect, gifts, charisma, good fortune, friends, family, or even character alone. You have to *live* life. Spiritually speaking, living IS the rule, not trying to live up to lifeless rules. The secret is to keep playing.

Nobody is going to get better at sports by completely modeling the methods and actions of someone else. They have to love the game. God is this same way but He is no game. With Him, we're playing for keeps. Remember that the phrase, *Law of God* has a few different usages in the Bible, so be careful not to confuse its meaning. Paul is actually clarifying something at the end of Romans 7 and the beginning of Romans 8 that has confused Christians for ages. He is teaching us that the spirit of the game of life, not its mechanics, is what wins. God cannot be followed mechanically any more than I can score like a professional just by emulating their movements. Delighting in the law of God is not the same as delighting in God, Himself (Romans 13:10).

The true law of God is that a person has to follow God for who He is, not for what they can get by associating with Him. He wants a people who will seek His face before His ways. The ways are very important, but they can mislead anyone who ends up following them at the expense of genuinely getting to know Him. This is the essence of why Adam and Eve yielded to the temptation of sin when God simply wanted them to keep eating from the Tree of Life and walking with Him every day. Since that time, sin has factored into every other human being's handicap, ourselves included.

Could it be that tragic things sometimes happen in our lives and communities because we claim association with a God on our own terms? If He were trying to warn us of calamity, would we hear? All the famous heroes of faith in the Bible were those who knew God's ways, but they were empowered, blessed, and became a blessing to others, because they knew Him. Paul discovered that no matter how much he wanted to serve God, there was something else working inside him against his own best intentions. Until we identify this same weak spot in ourselves, we will struggle as he did, with the frustrations that come from the spiritual friction acting upon our humanity.

"For what was impossible to the Law—powerless as it was because it acted through frail humanity (flesh)—God effected. Sending His own Son in a body like that of sinful human nature and as a sacrifice for sin, He pronounced sentence upon sin in human nature; in order that our case requirements of the Law might be fully met. For our lives are regulated not by our earthly, but by our spiritual natures." **Romans 8:3-4 WEY**

The law God gave Israel through Moses was like watching a pro play golf. It was His righteousness outlined in rules and regulations that would be natural for people who still lived in a Garden of

Eden state of spiritual life. The Ten Commandments along with hundreds of stipulations, were simply God's response to a people that did not wish to know Him on a day-to-day basis. Although He offered them a lifestyle that entailed food from Heaven and clothes that would not wear out, they constantly chose a religious approach to make up for their lifestyle of disobedience. Moses' law did one thing very well however, for a human race already fallen to the mercy of a sinful nature. It exposed sin as a problem that we cannot handle, making a Savior absolutely necessary.

It will help your future to remember Israel's past. When God saved them from Pharaoh (who is a type of Satan) and delivered them out of Egypt (which is a type of the world system), he did not do it based on a written law but on the blood of a sacrificial lamb (a type of Christ). Well before that, He had called Abram out of the heart of an ancient Babylonian society on the strength of a personal relationship, not a merit system. The only difference today is that we live on the opposite side of the cross. Jesus has become God's real provision for what was back then, only a promise.

We can win the fight and the match of life now, because the friction caused by sin has been compensated for in the blood of Jesus. The victory is factored into our score already, so we start way ahead of the game. God leveled the playing field by substituting a larger law, the law of the life that He lives, over the law of death that Satan fraudulently instituted on mankind. The Bible teaches that Jesus' death paid the legal death penalty that we had incurred, while simultaneously making God's own righteousness or goodness available to us for daily living.

The first Law of Spiritual Motion makes it possible for us to address our circumstances with God's purposes in mind. The Holy Spirit creates a greater force, within those who accept the responsibility of making Jesus the Lord of their lives, to use against the forces around them. We can step up and swing freely now, regardless of course conditions. The Spirit of Life in Christ, lifts us above the law that exposed our sins and held us in the devil's deadly

70

spiritual state. Like the Wright brothers using Newton's Law in reverse to invent flight, we are able to soar into limitless spiritual dimensions as a result of the unfathomable depths of the plan that God revealed in His Son.

"But in dealing with truths hitherto kept secret we speak of God's wisdom--that hidden wisdom which, before the world began, God pre-destined, so that it should result in glory to us; a wisdom which not one of the leaders of the present age possesses, for if they had possessed it, they would never have crucified the Lord of glory." **1 Corinthians 2:7-8 WEY**

Worldly minded thinkers are short sighted, not recognizing this higher set of spiritual laws at work dictating many of the natural things around them. The law of life we see operating in Jesus Christ affords access to a wisdom which is beyond that of both fallen man and fallen angels or spirits, to those who want to know. The Lord proved this repeatedly by walking on water, dismissing storms, turning water into wine, healing incurable diseases and controlling the demons in possessed people. It is only from this vantage point that we find our starting point. When we choose to think like God (according to His Word and Spirit) we can begin to move in directions that will change things in our world.

Jesus was able to step up to the circumstances that He faced in life and swing freely. His punches landed knockout blows, to the point that it almost seemed as if He was uncontested. After His resurrection, those human disciples who followed him for a mere three years, were able to do the same things, and even greater when you consider their corporate impact on the Roman world, in just a few short decades. What was the secret? Jesus imparted to them the same spiritual life source that He lived His life through, the Holy Spirit of God.

Get Your God-Waggle On!

I heard a professional golf instructor once describe a condition that was common to his students. He said that some people often freeze up when addressing the golf ball. Since they had a hard time starting their motion, he would devise ways for them to move before the move, so to speak. A 'waggle' is a common way to break the fear of thinking that you might fail, before your golf swing ever even starts. This is when a golfer moves the club around behind the ball a few times, practicing the address before settling the club down for the final swing. I think this analogy can help believers today activate what I call, Newtown's First Law of Motion.

By training yourself to act before taking the important actions in life, you can break the tendency to procrastinate when you feel a little of *Murphy's Law* creeping up on you. Why wait until it's too late to do something about the evil in your life or the darkness surrounding you in society? Develop a pre-shot routine that will get you used to moving forward with God and bring His goodness with you. Almost all professional golfers do this, so it is not that strange to have to fight the feelings of your old nature, even when you are highly experienced at engaging the new nature that Christ has died to give you access to.

Put this first law in motion immediately, even if you have to waggle to do it. The laws of physics say that we are going to stay in the state we are in, until something moves us in a different direction. Once you see the tremendous force behind what Jesus has done for all of us, your club should start moving. Sometimes that reminder is all you need to get headed in directions that will motivate many other people for good. Just think, if men like John Wycliffe, Johann Gutenberg, and William Tyndale hadn't moved to copy or print the first Bibles in their days, you probably wouldn't be reading this book right now.

In the military, they remove the pressure to act on important and sometimes scary orders by instituting *Standard Operating Procedures,* or *S.O.P.'s.* Many golf instructors use the same procedure when training their students to address the golf ball. They sometimes call it a *Pre-Shot Routine. It serves to* break everything down into smaller units, streamlining the process of accomplishing bigger tasks while making the overall result, more effective. Starting our day by giving God some time is a spiritual *S.O.P* that helps us deal with the problem of inertia. Seeking God's direction before making big decisions is a Pre-Shot Routine that helps us step up to the ball ready to make a calm, cool, quality swing.

The Apostle Paul discovered the laws of spiritual motion over 1500 years before Isaac Newton recognized their physical effects on planet earth and beyond. The higher nature of a true believer in Jesus Christ, truly frees that believer from the forces of human nature which were previously stuck in an inert state of spiritual being. This is why Paul could enter some of the darkest pagan cities of his day and disrupt the balance of spirituality there, until atmospheres conducive for revival broke out. If we could have been in places like Ephesus (Acts 19), we would have witnessed open spiritual warfare being waged as this short, poor-spoken preacher waggled his way to thousands of decisions for Christ. He certainly did not eliminate evil there, but we can clearly see what happened to the demographics in Ephesus, once waves of people started shifting from a position of spiritual darkness into God's light (Acts 19:19-27).

So, addressing spiritual inertia is the first answer to evil. Our motion has carried us to this tipping point that we face in society for reasons that must be responded to purposefully. The rest of Newton's laws of motion will be our simple outline for helping to remind us how to keep moving forward. Stop right here and get your spiritual waggle on, then put on your seatbelt. Once you become a doer of God's Word, all deception and delusion will move out, leaving more room for a powerful force in your life called faith.

CHAPTER SIX
Our 4th Move

THE 2nd LAW OF SPIRITUAL MOTION:
THE LAW OF FAITH

The 3 in 1 Law of Spiritual Motion

Before moving into this next law, let's first stop and restate the overall three step spiritual law of motion as found in scripture. Again, there are several passages that reflect this godly three in one principle, but this is maybe the most enlightening when it comes to dealing with evil:

"So be subject to God. Resist the devil [stand firm against him]. And he will flee from you." James 4:7 NLT

In our spiritual journey we initially move toward God, then with God, on our way to experiencing the movements of God back toward us. In the previous chapter we outlined the importance of beginning the process by moving to address God. We have actually discussed three steps overall that bring us up to this spiritual connecting point our next law provides. In preparation for "submitting" ourselves to God, remember to first decide you, 'want to know' spiritual realities and then choose to 'face the evil' that knowledge will present. Together our first three steps have equipped us to use the first law of spiritual motion, now we start throwing punches!

The 2nd Spiritual Law of Motion

Everyone and everything in life has potential, which is what Newton recognized in his Second Law of Motion. Again, it says, "A body's rate of change of momentum is proportional to the force causing it." In equation form it reads, 'F=ma,' meaning, force is the combination of mass multiplied by acceleration. This is the glue that connects initial movement with end result. It goes without saying that every moving mass in life has a specific potential for impact, depending on its size and the speed used to force its motion.

In other words, the kind of punch we 'pack', depends on the potential in the fist, arm, shoulder and body that we are throwing it with. Some boxers have knockout power, while others have to rely on the overall prowess of their technical skills to outpoint and outlast an opponent. Using our golf analogy, some players hit the ball very far while others are more dependent on the accuracy of their shot. We certainly need both power and precision but when we are first learning we just want to make solid contact.

Spiritually speaking, once we've moved to address our circumstances, we must take into consideration what the potential of our force is, to accelerate the mass that needs to be moved. Sometimes this refers to embracing the force of God's Holy Spirit to overcome the inert state that our human nature has become comfortable in. At other times, it means using it to move the obstacles that Satan has put in our way to hinder our progress in releasing the Kingdom of God around us.

My Second Law of Spiritual Motion refers to the knowledge of God that we need to navigate through the spiritual jungle that surrounds this natural world. It works on the heels of the first law, building a faith which grows out of contact with that Spirit of Life which is in the Lord. Once our lives are firmly invested in Him that same Spirit resides in us, giving us a greater strength to live life like Jesus. Consider how the following verses describe what His followers picked up about the secret of His connectivity which helped them direct their Christian approach to spirituality:

"But now God has shown us a way to be made right with him without keeping the requirements of the law (of Moses)...By what law? Of works? No, but by the law of faith (in Jesus Christ)." **Romans 3:21-27 NLT**

"For the sinful nature is always hostile to God. It never did obey God's laws, and it never will. That's why those who are still under the control of their sinful nature can never please God. But you are not controlled by your sinful nature. You are controlled by the Spirit if you have the Spirit of God living in you...And just as God raised Jesus from the dead, he will

give life to your mortal bodies by this same Spirit living within you." **Romans 8:7-11 NLT**

"Yet we have the same spirit of faith as he had who wrote, I have believed, and therefore have I spoken. We too believe, and therefore we speak, [Ps. 116:10.]" **2 Corinthians 4:13 AMP**

"And the Holy Spirit helps us in our weakness. For example, we don't know what God wants us to pray for. But the Holy Spirit prays for us...And the Father who knows all hearts knows what the Spirit is saying, for the Spirit pleads for us believers in harmony with God's own will. And we know that God causes everything to work together for the good of those who love God and are called..." **Romans 8:26-28 NLT**

"Now faith is a well-grounded assurance of that for which we hope, and a conviction of the reality of things which we do not see. For by it the saints of old won God's approval. Through faith we understand...that what is seen does not owe its existence to that which is visible...But where there is not faith it is impossible truly to please Him; for the man who draws near to God must believe that there is a God and that He proves Himself a rewarder of those who earnestly try to find Him." **Hebrews 11:1-6 WEY**

Like Newton's 2nd Law, this principle called, the "Law of Faith' teaches us that there is a real way to transfer energy from God's Kingdom into planet earth. Because of Jesus, the Holy Spirit instigates movements when working with the people of God which take the forces of heaven and apply them to our natural circumstances through two simple things, faith and prayer. The entire eleventh chapter of Hebrews illustrates the law of faith so clearly in recounting how even the godly 'heroes' of the Old Testament touched God by faith and then naturally touched people and things with that same energy of the Holy Spirit. The sincere motion we make toward God based on the sacrifice of His only Son, turns our potential into power to both change and to effect change around us.

Welcome to the Jungle

The more civilized we become, the more the 'Law of the Jungle' seems to apply in the most surprising areas of our modern society. Advancement in technology has created some great perks in life, but it certainly challenges us to solve a set of extreme problems that we've never had before. Because information is more attainable than ever, the experience to temper its misuse is naturally less available. Everybody has a smart phone today, yet our schools, the sector where we should be making the most intelligent progress, are sitting ducks for the most ignorant forms of violence. We find ourselves caught in an uneasy kind of 'twilight zone', where things feel like they are moving forward faster than ever before, yet we are growing more dependent on others to figure out where exactly it is that we're headed!

This is what the devil knew would happen way back in the garden. He knew that getting us to act independently without regard for the mechanics of God's leading, to want to know more at the expense of our character, would cost us the spiritual ability to manage this big blue ball as it moves through space. Given the fact that Newton discovered how connected time and motion really are, we can only imagine where we would be by this point, if we had followed God and allowed the positive laws of spiritual motion to keep rolling. We would've been living large and enjoying technologies long ago that we just now are beginning to realize have been ours all along!

When we step back and look at these tragic 'coincidental' convergences of evil in places like Sandy Hook, it all seems so unbalanced. Who could say that they enjoy putting their own children into this modern environment that we so confidently supervise? Now more than ever, it is like throwing them to the wolves and hoping for the best. I have a feeling that if we hadn't spent the past 50 years kicking God out of our national business, we wouldn't be getting many of the reactions we are receiving today. Be careful not to say that too loud, however, it might offend somebody about to unknowingly lose an innocent child in the next unsuspecting suburb somewhere!

If you haven't decided to fight back and defend your spiritual ground to save lives, instead of fearing the consequences of doing so and losing more of it, now is the time. This next spiritual law of motion is the important connector that allows our beginning movements to lead us to the right final outcomes, which restore the balance that Jesus died and rose for. According to Newton's 2nd Law, once we get into motion, we can then use the energy in play, to get the most out of our movements. The Law of Faith works the same way, rising up inside the person who makes the connection with God to believe what He says until it happens. The phrase, 'a moving vehicle is easier to steer,' describes how faith works with God's leading to apply some bigger and better solutions to the challenges of life's 'jungle,' regardless of what those challenges are.

Taking the Opportunity to Transfer Our Weight

After I recovered from my 6th grade drop in the ranks of the 'heaviest weights' of my early fighting career, I eventually restored my ego for a next level makeover. It turned out that my nemesis in elementary school lost his fight for a higher education and dropped out of school in junior high. With him gone, I still found myself in the 'jungle' of trying to figure out my way through life without a dad around to steer me in the right direction and to help provide the direction and momentum a young boy needs. There was still a fight deep inside me for reasons I didn't know how to explain, so I found a different way of entertaining it. The school we had graduated into was situated on a college campus across town and had built a reputation for epic fights in its many hidden locations like 'the gardens.'

In this setting, I discovered the less risky art of promoting fights between other, more willing participants, could help satisfy my inner warrior without having to actually fight myself. Getting someone else involved in the dirty work was half the pressure and twice the fun! As a seventh grader, I witnessed many awesome battles between the near men of our eighth and ninth grades. In these crowds, I soon resumed my tough talk and became a natural at getting other people in trouble. I was a risk taker at heart, so just knowing that we might all have to run from the authorities at any moment during these fights, became a rush I enjoyed. Along with being good at sports, these fights naturally helped me maintain the popular profile I had always been able to enjoy around school.

Looking back, this makes me think of the way churches today often look at the spiritual warfare raging before their eyes in their own cities. As a believer it is easy to forget that we are responsible for much of the spiritual action ourselves. If we hadn't answered the Lord's historic 'bell' and given our nation to Jesus in such an open way before the whole world, the devil would probably be much less inclined to so actively attack our sense of community. The problem is that we did it, overcoming obstacles and odds, fighting for freedoms and enjoying unbelievable success until, somewhere along the line, we began to take God's grace for granted, turning it into our own sense of entitlement. Even after that, we had a good run for a long time on reputation alone; just long enough to believe our past victories made us untouchable.

Like me as a kid, the church today suffers from the effects of unknowingly allowing circumstances to inflict just enough pain, causing it to transfer its gifts into the momentum of a crowd that promotes fights instead of winning them. The devil tricked Christianity here into erroneously thinking that it was America, until the country began to inform us again, that it is just another region of that old spiritually rebellious world system after all. Now we aren't sure whether we want to address the ball in front of us and play the course we live on or not. For the sake of tomorrow though, I am yelling at you like the old trainer in the *Rocky* movies, "get up, get up, get up!" After living through Newtown, I'm waving the smelling salts under the spiritual nose of this nation, before our senseless condition dictates that it is time for our corner to throw in the towel.

Of course, at 13 years of age I did not realize how an enemy that I didn't even know existed, kept pushing me dangerously close to losing sight of the right things I was born to fight for. I began to get the picture, however, the day that I felt as set of creepy, cold fingers grasp the back of my neck while watching another fight. I was standing just in view of the action, but positioned at a distance that I thought placed me just out of sight of any teachers or security personnel. To my horror, I had been caught off-guard by the principal of the school - with a principle of advice for me that would change my life. This guy had a reputation for dealing with issues and restoring order, which made the mere mention of his name a quick solution for most of the problems on campus. He didn't even stop the fight, he just told me something about this next spiritual law of motion.

"Rocky, I've heard of you," was Mr. P.'s surprising opening comment on my predicament. I didn't dare turn to look, I just listened and kept pretending to watch the fight. I knew him for sure, everybody did, but I was floored when I realized that he said he knew me?! "After watching you this year," he continued, "I want you to know that you have tremendous POTENTIAL to lead other people. Now, you can either choose to use what you have and set your course in life, or you can just get caught up going with the rest of the crowd."

I don't remember his exact words but that pretty much sums up what I got out of our face-to-back-of-the-head conversation. When I felt the release of his hand and finally had the courage to turn around, he was gone. I never had another conversation with Mr. P., he moved on himself after that year, but I never forgot what he shared with me. It made an impression, partially because it had been said to me by others before and partially because it would be reiterated to me again by the 'random' teacher here and there throughout the rest of my school career. Mostly, I couldn't forget it because it wasn't even really a conversation, it was a transfer of momentum, the result of a weighty principal using his position to force a little unexpected, but much needed, faith into my life.

A second spiritual law is coming at you like a fresh opportunity today. Maybe you are starting to realize that the heavenly Principal wants to have a chat? His very words inject faith into our hearts, even when there has been very little there before. His words leave lasting impressions that change our lives (Romans 10:17). When we don't listen, history teaches that we tend toward unfaithful things, leaving a lot of hopeless situations in our wake as a result. The great thing about the Bible is that it records the story of so many common, broken people who were in hopeless situations just like ours, until they made a faith connection with God.

I can make motion in life for good or evil, depending on my intentions and choices. Mr. P. decided to use what he had, to transfer opportunity to a young boy with no faith to figure it out by himself. He was betting on the fact that I would be a willing receptor for his wisdom and that the kinetic energy of that transfer, would go a long way with the potential he saw in me and in my future. It had a profound natural impact. More importantly, we can make motion with the much greater power of God and get supernatural results in life, which can do more than compensate for evil actions, it can stop their source!

The Secret to All Spiritual Success

Again, Jesus is our main model for all things spiritual, then the examples of those who followed in His footsteps. He demonstrated the transfer of energy in several ways. First, when Jesus needed to 'recharge' His batteries He did so by going to God in prayer. Second, the transfer He received from God He was also able to give out to those around Him. The kinds of things the Lord said and did were not of His own human making. They were the things put into His heart and soul by his interaction with his heavenly Father. When He gave God's words out, the Holy Spirit moving in and around His life transferred not only the directions but also the spiritual power behind them. This is why Jesus was able to command demons, effect people and change circumstances at times in miraculous ways.

"Come close to God, and God will come close to you..."
James 4:8a NLT

Spiritual cause and effect begins to work through something called, 'prayer.' It is the vehicle which brings the most important part of our being before the Lord: the heart. We tend to look at circumstances and people through the lens of our physical eye, but the Bible says that God looks first at the heart (1 Samuel 16:7). To Him, every situation starts there, then truth is discerned before His spiritual eyes. Prayer is the tool that God gives us so that we can keep a spiritual eye on reality as well and get the God-transfers we need for success in life.

In the Bible, "prayer" takes several similar but different forms which lend to our fuller understanding of its meaning. When first used in Genesis 20:7 & 17, it refers to "intercession" or standing in the space between God and someone else, asking for His help. Prayer is usually thought of as starting with us but it can be surprisingly initiated by God, so we have to stay ready. When God prepared to judge the conditions at Sodom and Gomorrah He first unexpectedly visited Abraham to discuss the situation. When this happened Abraham responded and "drew near" to God to negotiate terms (Genesis 18:23). Whether we start the praying or God leads us to do so, we should always be prepared to move spiritually, knowing it will cause Him to respond even more!

God is like that. He wants us to keep the conversation open with Him so He can transfer things into our hearts that will further the movement of His will in the earth. These cities were going to be judged but the Lord wanted to teach us how to work with Him even in the worst situations to bring out the good. Notice how Abraham instinctively knew what to do. He immediately began prying into God's mind, looking for loopholes and asking for righteous mercy.

In the New Testament, the most common word for prayer simply means to "make forward motion toward God." 1 Timothy 2:1 tells us to do this on behalf of all men, especially ruling authorities, in the form of petitions or requests, intercession or interviews like Abraham conducted and with gratitude. To pray means all these things but most importantly it means to get into spiritual motion. Abraham didn't save the cities but he saved his family members in those cities from destruction. Two other Old Testament leaders,

Joshua and Hezekiah, literally turned time backward as a result of the intensity of their movements toward God (Joshua 10:13-14; 2 Kings 20:9-11)!

The Mass That Prayer Accelerates

So, what is it that prayer carries to makes it so potentially powerful? The answer is such an obvious and overused term in religious language today that we easily read right past it, if we do pick up the Bible.

"I tell you, you can pray for anything, and if you believe that you've received it, it will be yours." **Mark 11:24 NLT**

There is a spiritual substance that carries tremendous potential for change in this physical world. It is called 'faith.' The power it carries is the energy of God's Holy Spirit, potent enough to change the nature of any man, regardless of the wilderness or jungle he finds himself in. We all know by living with ourselves on this planet that if something can do that, nothing else should be impossible! Faith is a law, which when carried into motion through prayer can reverse the evil effects of sin in the heart of any situation and leave it right in the very sight of God.

The law of Moses could never do that. At its best, removed from the knowledge of God Himself, it just made people more aware of the sin in their lives, condemning them to a kind of religious guilt and stuck in the inertia created by their dead spiritual state. When Israel prided themselves as the keepers of the perfect law of God, it only deluded them further into believing they had something 'they' could do with which to boast about. In reality, they could not measure up to its heavenly standard in their sin-damaged human condition. Religion can do that to anyone, even us, if we don't stop and realize that our confidence has to be in the Lord Who is willing to save our souls and deliver us from evil. That, my friend, is the heart attitude that can only come from knowing God...that is the law of faith!

When the kids in your sleepy little town or suburb start getting murdered for no good reason you know you've got a mountain of evil on your hands that religion, mere spirituality or good intentions can't do anything about. It can, however, point us to a supernatural movement shifting across the horizon of time, calling for a genuine faith that does reverse curses when they come (Proverbs 26:2). It is more than interesting that both Jesus and Moses at their births seemed to spark a flurry of evil activity directed at killing the children in their surroundings. This was, no doubt, an attempt by Satan to kill them and God's plan for both their own generations and the subsequent spiritual reverberations of goodness these key figures would generate throughout all time.

We know it did not work either time and I'm telling you it doesn't have to work in your surroundings either (Exodus 1:16, 22; Matthew 2:16). There continue to be shootings around the country while I am working on this book. The one in Newtown still feels different though, like a specific marker signifying a 'new' battle for 'towns' and territories everywhere. The hurricane that preceded Sandy Hook put an emphasis on this one event that is hard for any prophetic eye to miss. Satan is letting us know once again that he is willing to force the issue and try to steal God's thunder.

Therefore, we have to be willing to use the only force at our disposal which can defeat evil in the human race, faith. Specifically, the kind that comes from multiple hearts united in prayer behind God's higher plans. We catch glimpses of its greatness by remembering past battles and applying the approach of godly people in other times to our current events. For example, Moses had the benefit of faithful parents in his house to save him and God had many faithful midwives working together throughout the land to save other children in his day. Jesus also had faithful parents and the map of Moses' Law, with all its hidden markers known as 'types and shadows' (Colossians 2:17; Hebrews 8:5).

Plus, the Messiah had the power of all the words of the Old Testament's prophets, which guided an unusually wise group of men from afar to believe and act on his behalf as a child. They not only helped signal the shift the skies were already revealing but also thwart the enemy's encroachments. When God called Abraham, He even initially proved his faithfulness by testing his willingness to sacrifice his own son, like many of his contemporaries did to their false gods. With Adam it was a faith test to restrict the one tree which would prevent Eve's children from living their lives in God's garden. When David stumbled in faith, it cost him the faithfulness of his children for generations.

Both Adam and Abraham had previously lived beyond the clutches of evil by walking with God in faith. It even demanded faith for Moses to answer his call, receive the Law of God and deliver it as written testimony to the perfection of God Almighty before a hopelessly faithless group of 'believers' destined to wander around in the wilderness until they died. David and the prophets understood the importance of this faith relationship while living under Moses' Law, which is what set them apart and gave them insight into the future. Jesus embodied it all as God in human form, but He specifically restored this original higher Law of Faith for living and modeled it for the world to grasp.

Faith for the Final Push

I think it is increasingly becoming clear that we are moving into a final era where the devil is quickly gathering his world to take one last swing at stopping the only spiritually qualified group Jesus said would be his downfall. These are those of us who will believe enough to gather ourselves in God's Spirit and use the keys He gives us to move with Him in heavenly places (see the final chapter). The true Church is the only entity on planet earth authorized to stop the gates of hell by creating bigger openings to God's goodness (Matthew16:18). Therefore, we need to awaken the prayer warriors and defenders of real faith in preparation for His return. That is why we, like others before us, have been given access to this difference maker the Bible calls the 'spirit of faith.'

"Yet we have the same spirit of faith as he had who wrote, I have believed, and therefore have I spoken. We too believe, and therefore we speak, [Ps. 116:10.]" **2 Corinthians 4:13**

I love knowing that the 116th Psalm, quoted here, has an unknown author. It wasn't one of the great men God raised up for an important spiritual shift in history, but rather just an 'anybody' like you and me. The lesson is, when we believe, God we can make a difference at any point in time. Faith has the power through prayer to make us super-human in very real ways. Not only can we swing a big spiritual club but we are supposed to swing for the fences once we have learned to "draw near to God!"

"Is anyone among you afflicted (ill-treated, suffering evil)? He should pray...And the prayer of faith will save him who is sick, and the Lord will restore him; and if he has committed sins, he will be forgiven...The earnest (heartfelt, continued) prayer of a righteous man makes tremendous power available [dynamic in its working]." James 5:13-16 AMP

Tremendous power flows through the prayer of any man who gets right with the Lord and takes big swings from the heart! The 'prayer of faith' can save, heal, cast devils out, overcome incredible odds and even move giant obstacles according to the Bible. If we read it more often we would pounce on evil more readily when it shows its ugly face. "Tremendous power" describes the kind of energy that can move objects on a spiritual level like Newton described in the motion of a physical object. Prayer is no insignificant exercise...it is actually choosing to say what God says back to Him in anticipation of making big impacts.

"Who by [the help of] faith subdued kingdoms, administered justice, obtained promised blessings,..." Hebrews 11:33

"Then Jesus said to the disciples, 'Have faith in God. I tell you the truth, you can say to this mountain, 'May you be lifted up and thrown into the sea,' and it will happen. But you must really believe it will happen and have no doubt in your heart. I tell you, you can pray for anything, and if you believe that you've received it, it will be yours. Mark 11:22-24 NLT

Notice the words, "say," "pray," heart, "faith," "doubt" "believe" and "receive" here. They go together in spiritual life to either act or quit at the bottom of the problematic mountains we face. In this story, Jesus had just cursed a fig tree, one of the only negative and judgmental displays of God's power attributed to His faith. If you read the previous verse you will find that the Lord did this by speaking alone. Faith can be a prayer but because it is a spiritual act can be more particularly described as giving voice to the heart.

If you've read the four Gospel accounts of Jesus' life, Matthew, Mark, Luke and John, you probably know He regularly super-ceded the natural laws of physics and usually did it to help someone in trouble. He never once used the 'tremendous power' of the Holy Spirit to inflict physical harm on anyone. He did go around "doing good and healing all that were oppressed of the devil" (Acts 10:38). He did give people the benefit of their doubtful condition by announcing the good news of God to them, that Heaven's Kingdom was available for the taking. Jesus often used His faith to compassionately help both individuals or groups of thousands who had little of their own.

Jesus especially responded to this substance called faith when he found the slightest evidence of it in a person. He once used the power of God to walk across a lake for no apparent reason and then invited Peter to join the fun and do the same by engaging his own faith! In ten particular cases, Jesus directly told individuals that they had received a miracle because, "their faith" had touched something of God's nature and made them well. When prayer puts faith into spiritual motion, dynamic, and otherwise unbelievable, things begin to happen.

Faith is used the same way God originally used it in creating the universe, He simply "said' and it happened. Jesus mirrored this in His life and ministry teaching us to believe and then speak to situations that need to be restored by God's power. It is impossible to miss the fact that He used faith on circumstances and also "against" evil. Jesus continually cast demons out of people wherever He encountered them, the first but not the last time being in the synagogues or churches of His time and culture (Luke 4:33). It is important to recognize how they often "cried out" for Jesus to leave them alone in a similar fashion to those who by faith "cried out" to Jesus for help.

The words used by these people in the Bible teach us what we have to do before our opportunities pass us by. Prayer is the backswing that positions your spiritual golf club to swing in faith. Friction will scream at you to stop, tell you that you're not strong enough or tempt you to pull your head up and take your eyes off the ball. This is where you have to get 'louder' than a cheated widow with nowhere else to turn (Luke 18:7) and 'crazier' than two blind men chasing a healer and croaking like ravens. (Matthew 9:27)! These are the pictures the Bible paints for us to describe faith that moves all obstacles in its way. (see words translated, "cry" and "crying" in the aforementioned verses, Strong's Exhaustive Concordance of the Bible.)

Only the Strong Survive

Jesus explained, in Luke 11:14-26, how these things work from a spiritual perspective. One spiritual force is stronger than another, and when pitted against each other the stronger will prevail. The secret of Jesus' successful faith, powerful prayers and bold voice was that He was stronger in spirit than any demon or circumstance He encountered. His potential in God was weightier, His energy more kinetic and the acceleration of the Holy Spirit faster than anything coming at Him. This is not to say His battles were easy or insignificant.

It is equally as true that Jesus' disciples did the same works He did in all these same arenas with the same results. They not only overcame the same things but in even greater levels because they had the luxury of a united power which came through putting all their individual prayer and faith together! Jesus captured the attention of Israel in His day, his Church full of believers captured the entire Roman Empire in 300 years and is well on its way to having prepared the whole world for Jesus' return in just under 2000! Like Jesus said, nothing is impossible with God and because that is true, nothing is impossible with anyone with the strength that comes from believing it (Matthew 17:20; 19:26)!

The only reason today that we can't handle the evil in our own "Christian" country is because we struggle to stay strong enough spiritually to believe. Most people in Newtown will put this book down once they read the word, "Satan" even though one of the centers for the "Church of Satan" is located right here in this same town!

The way to stay strong is to pray and to feed yourself a steady diet of what God says i.e. the Bible. By doing this your faith will grow in step with your increasing spiritual maturity and the power of spiritual motion will move through you. When enough people do this together a larger momentum and the kind of spiritual insulation recorded in "The Acts of the Apostles" starts to develop. The Apostle Paul went to the dark city of Ephesus on a mission trip and only spent two years there before demons were manifesting and witches were burning their most expensive books in public (Acts 19:1-23)!

Of course there is a price to pay for making motion toward God and stopping evil in the streets. Paul was also imprisoned, stoned, slandered and forsaken by friends and fellow believers. His secret was a relentless faith that just kept swinging with the forces of God anyway. It accelerated him into the highest courts and made him a voice before kings and masses. We are not shocked and overwhelmed bystanders; we are today's extension of that earliest Church, God's very capable 'spiritual first responders!'

CHAPTER SEVEN
Our 5th Move

THE 3RD LAW OF SPIRITUAL MOTION: THE LAW OF GROWTH

The 3-in-1 Law of Spiritual Motion

We have finally come to the 3rd Law of Spiritual Motion. This is the law that all the other laws work toward. In Newton's Law, this is the one that everybody remembers because this is where the payoff is. So, before explaining the final part of our three part spiritual law of motion, let's reread the Bible verse upon which it is based and do a quick review.

"So be subject to God. Resist the devil [stand firm against him]. And he will flee from you." **James 4:7 NLT**

Newton's 1st Law of Motion says that we have to break the balance of inertia to get movement started or stopped. There is a natural tendency in all objects to resist change, so an unbalanced force is required to change their resistance to a new direction. Our spiritual counterpart says that we have to act before we think too much and talk ourselves into accepting less than God's best. We will have to break spiritual complacency to effectively address our situation. If we're lazy or passive, we need a wake-up call. If we're riding high on life's roller coaster we'd better buckle up. We have to find our waggle.

Newton's 2nd Law takes us one step further so that we can connect, to eventually get the result that we're looking for. It reminds us that all objects that we face are not equal, and teaches us that we will need increasingly more force to accelerate heavier things. After all, it takes more strength to move a mountain than a molehill. On the spiritual side, we learned that the prayer of faith gives us an advantage. This substance can make us equal to any weight that we may have to move, or use any friction trying to stop us in the process. Amazingly, we can move either a mountain or a mulberry tree (Mark 11:23; Luke 17:6) with only the smallest amounts of this heavenly heft that God has sparks within us, to be used for our spiritual well-being.

The Third Law of Spiritual Motion

When we begin to think about how our 3rd law of spiritual motion works in real time, we must first factor in all the variables involved in our heavenly vision. Following the Lord is not easy, just because we can break it into a few bullet points but it pays off big-time. Of course, in all reality, there are more variables here than modern quantum physics has added to Newton's Law or will add as technology expands. Only God, in His infinite wisdom, knows all the secrets of time, space, and eternity, but we must be responsible with the ones that we know. Jesus said it this way:

"And if you do not carry your own cross and follow me, you cannot be my disciple. But don't begin until you count the cost. For who would begin construction of a building without first calculating the cost to see if there is enough money to finish it?" **Luke 14:27-28 NLT**

The 3rd Law of Spiritual Motion is the finisher. Once we choose to know and get going, it will ensure that we are rewarded. We can know what to expect, to a large degree in life, because this law dictates that everything that will happen is governed by what has happened or is happening. We all have free will, so counting the cost upfront is important; it tells us what we can expect next. Newton's 3rd Law of Motion states, "For every action there is an equal and opposite reaction." This is the reaction force we get in exact response to every force that moves. It is equal in size, but opposite in direction, which is actually quite scriptural.

"Don't be misled-you cannot mock the justice of God. You will always harvest what you plant. Those who live only to satisfy their own sinful nature will harvest decay and death from that sinful nature. But those who live to please the Spirit will harvest everlasting life from the Spirit. So let's not get tired of doing what is good. At just the right time we will reap

a harvest of blessing if we don't give up." **Galatians 6:7-9 NLT**

In this universe, whenever an object pushes another object, it gets pushed back in the opposite direction but equally as hard. Here on earth, we sometimes refer to the emotional sensation of this effect as *backlash*. When you're joyriding through life and hit a wall, what you feel the next day is referred to as *whiplash*. When this principle is put into common language like these two words, it becomes very applicable since we've all been lashed more times and in more ways than most of us can remember. It starts at conception. If you weren't aborted by someone else's dark decision to play God and redirect you to Heaven without His or your permission, you were eventually delivered into this world through a shocking emergence into a new reality called, birth. It is simply the logical reaction to what your parents planted in intimacy, several months before.

However hard we punch determines the amount of damage done to our opponent. How hard, fast, and accurately we swing the golf club determines the quality of the shot that our ball will reflect, hopefully in the fairway or on the green ahead of us. When we pull the trigger in life, we need to already have known something about the gun that we're using. The kickback we are going to feel in our wrists or shoulder, will be in direct proportion to the size or caliber of the bullet in our chamber. If you're not ready for it, you might be in for a shock. Because of this law, most hunters remember the first time they fired a shotgun. When the gun is pointed in the wrong direction we all remember it!

When one force pushes toward another, one gets pushed back. Spiritually, we are going to reap exactly what we plant according to a law of reproduction. We either sow God's goodness in accordance with the law of the Spirit of Life (which produces a spirit of prayer and faith as a result of His love for us), or we perpetuate evil in accordance with the law of the Spirit of Sin and Death, living only to enjoy the pleasures of this world system which is operated courtesy of the devil, who hates us all. Either way we are going to get the effect that we ourselves cause on varying levels, reaping what we plant in the fields of our lives, families, cities and nations. Seeds that are planted and nurtured properly grow.

Wrestling for Your Blessings

When I got to high school, I found the best physical outlet for the fighting spirit I seemed to have been born with. The wrestling team presented an outlet for me to be a tough guy, legally. Blending my love for sports with my need to battle, the gym mat became the surface on which I learned to grind out some of my root issues that Mr. P. and others had helped point out. Gaining discipline and eradicating some of the inconsistencies that the lack of discipline had produced in me, helped prepare me for the biggest victory of my life, to date. Looking back, it also showed me how working with this final law of motion, paid off in bigger ways than I had learned in any physics class.

Wrestling is a perfect mixture of individual accomplishment and teamwork, each being just as important as the other. It is also a spiritual act of aggression, recommended in the Bible that reaps rewards (Genesis 32:24-30). For me, being introduced to this sport was too good to be true at this point; it was perfect timing. Wrestling really was an unexpected reaction to many of the motions made in my life up until that time. It seemed to me, nothing could have been better than getting trained to fight in a legally controlled environment. Plus, I was allowed to miss a little school on the side so I was all in!

That is why it was so disappointing when my old number-one enemy, pinned me unexpectedly just when the fun was getting started. A younger, weaker teammate was somehow able to defeat me when we wrestled against each other for a spot on the varsity team. Just like the kid I had fought in elementary school years earlier, there seemed to be no good reason for my loss. In fact, it seemed I had physically outperformed both of my opponents on each occasion, yet somehow was left shamefully beaten in the end. Starting is a problem sometimes when it comes to using motion to our advantage in life, but finishing well is the toughest thing to learn *most* of the time.

My problem was never physical, even though I was always one of the smallest kids in my class. What I lacked in size, I was able to make up in ability, charisma, and popularity, which is why I always found a way to make a comeback. If you could somehow look back in time, you would find that these embarrassingly huge losses that I'm telling you about, barely registered on most of my classmates' minds. In fact, it would probably seem as if I had most things going for me (with the exception of a father to keep me pointed in the right direction). My problem wasn't physical, but mental; I realized this problem only when I started fighting as hard with my head as I had been with my fists. This was the only way I could stop beating myself in life's key moments.

It wasn't until I got around the environment of team and coach, in a setting I could appreciate, that I found the missing side of me that was willing to win, regardless of setbacks and cost. In a relatively short period of time, I learned to let go of some personal negatives and focus on being a better thinker, so that I could help advance the cause of my teammates. I had been on winning teams before, and I had fought more successful fights than not, but the convergence of the two was a watershed moment in my young life. This switch made me better at wrestling as well as a lot of other things. My junior and senior years became quite successful, the highlight of which was being named co-captain of that team.

In one year, surprisingly enough to me and my teachers, the mental discipline also bled into my studies, making me an A-student. In two particular classes, literature and history, I did so well that my instructors often just stared at me during class because they were so surprised. My reputation had preceded me, so they knew my record and had every right to be suspiciously shocked. One of them had failed me in Spanish class, just the year before. I even received another invitation, this time from Principal J., to discuss the importance of increasing my class load in preparation for college.

This little insight into the progression of my life as a warrior-in-the-making might not mean as much to you, but I know how well it worked to get me to another level, practically speaking. Best of all and unbeknownst to me, it was also preparing me to take an even higher step. This is why I think it's really important for people everywhere, especially Christians, to revisit the spiritual aspect of life's movements today. After all, we are speeding through the universe on a massive ball, spinning in circular motion with all the power of tremendous kinetic and potential energies. What's more, as a unit we are working our way through a universe filled with other objects, circling other objects, circling other objects.

The point is, we need to connect with where we are going. It is better if we get ahead of the game by learning how motion works and then planning to work with it. I have simplified the details and changed names to protect the innocent people who had to put up with me, but all the elements that God gives to create real change are in my little fight story. These elements are also in the sports examples that I have given you. Most importantly, however, this principle is in our Bibles and it works in our hearts, by the power of the Holy Spirit, to help transfer the faith to unlock God's potential around us. He knows exactly where we're going.

You Gotta Fight for Your Right to Finish

It is easy to stop short in life and call your territory 'big enough', because the fight to increase is difficult. That nasty law of sin and death described in Romans, ensures natural things tend to work entropically, decreasing the other energies that impede its own increase. We naturally cool down even after we've been on fire for a cause, so we have to stop every so often and recount the costs to move ahead. My purpose for writing this book is to bring as many people as read it, to that place with the Lord. Pause and consider whether you have really looked at the circumstances around you and the circumstances inside you. If you decide to go through the motions to save others by stopping evil, God has to be able to first stop and save you.

When I graduated from high school in the summer of 1983, I was already a new man in so many ways, but I hadn't yet completely connected with my real purpose. As I prepared my college entrance paperwork, excited by the events that had led to my high school turn-around, I thought I was ready to take on the world. It would have been easy for me to chart my course into adulthood, based on all the good things that had happened over the course of my last two years. I believe I would have done well moving in any direction because I had made the necessary first moves to get productive results. The one thing I wouldn't yet do was the thing that God wanted me to do, however.

Looking back, I'm so glad He would not leave me alone until I thought more deeply about fighting to cross that finish line that I somehow knew would prepare me to soar in life. I've given the Lord all the credit in this book because He was the 'one more move' that I needed to make, to seal the divine reaction to the many previous actions He had initiated in my life. It was this 'something else' feeling that was stirring in me, beneath the surface of all these other events needing to be addressed before I could become a true spiritual champion. To make a long story short, I won the final victory by finally losing the most important fight of my life—the fight to say 'no' to the Lord's call.

You need to lose that same fight if you are going to win in life. As we mentioned, He holds the science behind the Law of Life that was and is displayed in Christ Jesus. He is what you get for stepping up to the spiritual plate and using the Law of Faith. What else could you want or need? If I can get you to connect with Him, the only one who strikes out is Satan. Satan no longer gets to use you for his purposes anymore, even if it is just to wink at the evil on your block. He doesn't get to spend an eternity of hell with you either.

He gets the Hell out, while God moves Heaven in, literally. You see, your saying yes to Him, is the reaction to all those moments in your life that have brought you to this moment. God has been moving over the dark waters of your past, speaking words of life and shining light into your heart, when you didn't even realize it was Him. He has done it to keep the law of spiritual motion working to bring you to a point of realization now. For some of you it is a first and final decision to repent of your association with sin and death so that you can experience the sensation of the spirit of true life.

Other readers need to come back to that place personally and reconnect with Jesus so that other people can connect for the first time with His heavenly protection, provision, and promotion.

The devil has maintained such a sketchy and scary reputation that people either don't think they need to deal with him, or are simply afraid to. What you must understand about him more than anything else however, is the one thing that scares him the most. He can't help but remember the scriptural truth most believers today have so easily forgotten. If you submit yourself to God and resist the devil, the way spiritual authority moves through a believer produces a terrifying reaction in him, like it or not. Satan doesn't want his real reputation getting out because he knows when it does, a lot more of his activity in the heavenlies will be grounded, while God's servants will soar to new heights.

Sit Back, Buckle Up, and Enjoy the Flight

The sensation that we feel upon takeoff from our local airport illustrates the meaning of equal but opposite better than anything. What the pilot puts into the throttle is exactly what we get out of the ride, just with a reverse sensation. The thrust of the jet's engine pushes against the mass of air behind it, which has a natural push-back effect, propelling the aircraft forward. Every time I get on a flight, I love to feel the process of forces working against each other, pushing me places I could never go on my own. I get there faster, avoid the friction of traveling on the ground, and have so much more fun doing it.

This ability to fly when everyone was walking, is what made Jesus such an interesting character to so many people. Think about it. He is more famous today than He ever has been. That's because He broke all of the laws that other people have to obey, for all the right reasons. His ability to be naturally supernatural has the world still asking questions today. Finding answers is as simple as reading Jesus' own words—the ones printed in loud red ink in many Bibles, so they stand out and we can't miss them.

Jesus did really crazy stuff sometimes, but He did mind-blowing things all the time. As I mentioned earlier, He broke the natural laws of physics walking on water and turning water into wine. He also disappeared into thin air, transported through time and space, commanded storms to cease, multiplied food at least twice and told fishermen how and where to make miracle catches a few other times. Beyond these, Jesus regularly healed the sick, cleansed people from their sin, and most importantly to our theme here, cast demons out of people's lives. Sometimes all of these things were connected spiritually in a certain situation, while at other times, each was a miracle of its own particular kind.

Jesus was simply amazing, but what amazes me even more than His incredible story is people's ability to read right past most of it. In fact, the amazement itself seems to often be the problem. Like the shock we feel when tragedy strikes, there is a certain fear factor associated with things outside what is familiar to us. It is the opposite extreme of what happens when we become over-familiar, but with the same results—we check out of reality (Matthew 13:53-58; Mark 5:14-18). We must be careful not to unknowingly demand that God remain so understandable to us all the time. Notice some of the people's responses to Jesus in His own day:

"The disciples were absolutely terrified. 'Who is this man?' they asked each other. 'Even the wind and waves obey him!'" **Mark 4:41 NLT**

"Amazed, the people exclaimed, 'What authority and power this man's words possess! Even evil spirits obey him, and they flee at his command!'" **Luke 4:36 NLT**

"When the Temple guards returned without having arrested Jesus, the leading priests and Pharisees demanded, 'Why didn't you bring him in?' 'We have never heard anyone speak like this!' the guards responded.'" **John 7:46-47 NLT**

"As Jesus said 'I Am he,' they all (Judas and all the temple guards coming to arrest Him) drew back and fell to the ground!" **John 18:6 NLT**

"They were completely amazed and said again and again, 'Everything he does is wonderful. He even makes the deaf to hear and gives speech to those who cannot speak.'" **Mark 7:37 NLT**

The Law of the God's Land

This spiritual law of motion reminds me of another familiar old saying that you sometimes hear in American culture. The *Law of the Land,* was legal language used to civilize our country's wilderness territories. Since injustice was a given in places like the wild west, where people often had to police themselves, this concept was adopted to refer to the right of every man to survive the natural *Law of the Jungle* that we discussed in the last chapter. It gave everyone fair protection by granting them the right to a fair judgment in court by their own peers. So justice would prevail during the expansion of this nation (it often did not anyway, when neither the letter nor the spirit of the law were obeyed), in 1787 early American policymakers borrowed this phrase from wording in the "Magna Carta."

The Continental Congress used the same language that many of their own ancestors had used 500 years prior to shape English law. Our founding fathers issued the Northwest Ordinance, a legal document providing rules for governing territories outside the boundaries of the organized United States. More so than that, we are all familiar with the similar clause 'due process', written into the language of the United States Constitution. Both of these phrases represent how push back works in community. When people begin to cooperate in standing for justice, the injustice naturally resident in the human race, cannot so easily prevail. Thank God that the positive side of this 3rd law has been moving around in our politics and law enforcement circles for hundreds of years to thwart many of the negative forces that we have faced from both within and without.

Doing the right thing goes a long way in society because it is one of the ways that humans act like God. In the three-in-one manifestation of God in the Bible (Father, Son, Holy Spirit), there are so many attributes describing His goodness. When we begin to plant God in our hearts, so many good things can come out of us. For example: God is Love, when we are led by His Spirit, the love of God begins to manifest in and around us. Jesus is the Way, when we follow Him, ways open for us and for others. The Holy Spirit is the heavenly Advocate, Teacher and Guide. When we push into His help, wisdom and direction come back to us. This is the law of God's land, so to speak, the law of the spirit of how He created everything to move.

I listened recently as Dr. Michio Kaku give a talk on his "Big Think" video series about the amazing advances being made in the realm of optics. He described a super camera developed at MIT, which is able to capture one trillion frames per second. This kind of technology is rapidly changing the way that we will be able to see reality in and around us. He related how the human brain is bound to think at the speed of the chemical reactions that make up its processes. However, life really does go on beyond that limited scope at two extremes, both of which we cannot normally see. Inner space can happen on this scale of trillionths of a second, while outer space has the potential of spanning trillions of years. This teaches us that what we see naturally is not the only thing being seen. What is going on beyond our capability to see is outside of our limited mental frame of reference...but what God sees is always right and right on time!

Hopefully, little factoids like that can help expand our minds to the realities of the things that God has said all along and open our hearts to bigger possibilities in the realm of supernatural technologies. Jesus and His disciples often used these godly realities to win their worlds. Sadly, the devil will use science to mislead many into factoring God out of their life equations, but I want you to know that we can have some huge micro and macro breakthroughs in our realities, if we just dare to believe. After all, God created the natural realm so the supernatural is only at arm's length, at a speed just beyond our usual comprehension. (Luke 17:20-21) I don't know the shutter speed a camera would need to have to capture Heaven and Hell, but I know the human heart has the capacity to see what cannot be seen and to change things, through the spirit of faith, that cannot otherwise be changed (check out how God's *Law of Liberty* helps us see, James 1:22-25).

God's Kingdom = Spiritual Force

Big time God-reactions are just waiting on big time believers to make the first moves. Jesus Christ is not just an amazingly different kind of man, He was the technology of God's first move to restore His kingdom to mankind. God has already moved and, through His Son, already done everything necessary to remove everything Satan did to unbalance things and tip them in his dark direction. Therefore, in many ways, God is waiting on us. Where are the seers of old to show the way to new heights? They are around I assure you, but what we don't realize is many of them are us.

We need to step out toward the areas that God has called us to influence and start unlocking spiritual doors with the Keys of God's Kingdom. If we reconnect with our Creator, we will be given these keys, and if we let Him reconnect us properly with each other, we will learn to effectively use them. If we compare Matthew 16:18-19 with 18:18-19, we find something amazing about our own God-given ability to govern His territory here on earth.

"I will build my church, and all the (gates) powers of hell will not conquer it. And I will give you the keys of the Kingdom of Heaven. Whatever you forbid on earth will be forbidden in heaven, and whatever you permit on earth will be permitted in heaven.'" Matthew 16:16-19 NLT

"'I tell you the truth, whatever you forbid on earth will be forbidden in heaven, and whatever you permit on earth will be permitted in heaven. I also tell you this: If two of you agree here on earth concerning anything you ask, my Father in heaven will do it for you.'" Matthew 18:18-19 NLT

We have the ability to affect the bigger spaces around us when we respect His important spaces within and between us. The authority to literally *permit* and *forbid* is more than most us probably want to take responsibility for but think about the implications. We already know that there is a big task before us, but in God we're equal to it and He has put others around us to make these spiritual laws even more powerful in accomplishing His will through us. We will end the book talking about the latter, but let's complete this chapter discussing the former.

I came up with *Newtown's Law* to point out the spiritual storm that is brewing. Like in Jesus' day, these things start in the heavenly realm, but they eventually get down to boots on the ground, right where we live. When the devil brings the battle to us, we have to bring it back to him or get marched over. When he tempted Jesus in the wilderness, it was an illustration showing us how to win the original battle that Adam and Eve lost. Satan tried to dictate, but Jesus merely inserted God's Word, the Bible, between Himself and His enemy. In short order, the devil did what he always has to do— he cut his losses and ran in hopes of finding another, more opportune season to inject his half-truths and lies into the strange new human side of the divine mind. When he tried again, God lured him back into another garden, the Garden of Gethsemane, where the results this time were his own entrapment in a divine plan that led to his complete defeat.

This shows us how to wage successful warfare from the beginning of our callings, to the end. Satan is not as good at raising hell as he once was, but if we don't know what Jesus did to him, he can seem as good as he ever was. Taking him out depends on our taking into consideration both what has happened and what is happening. Our spiritual outcomes are the result of knowing the past tense of God's promises, and then moving present tense with what He wants done. This kind of pressing spiritual violence is what Jesus said takes the kingdom of God by force.

"...the kingdom of heaven has endured violent assault, and violent men seize it by force [as a precious prize]. A share in the heavenly kingdom is sought with most ardent zeal and intense exertion." **Matthew 11:12 AMP**

"Then God made you alive with Christ, for he forgave all our sins. He canceled the record of the charges against us and took it away by nailing it to the cross. In this way, he disarmed the spiritual rulers and authorities, He shamed them publicly by his victory over them on the cross." **Colossians 2:13-15 NLT**

There it is again, this law of spiritual motion is everywhere in scripture. Jesus never sat around waiting to respond to the devil, He simply kept pouring on the pressure of a life responding to God. You will notice in the four Gospels how Jesus *rebuked* whatever did not belong in His way. The word rebuke meant *to tax upon* in the original language. Whether it was sickness, demonic activity, or misguided believers, Jesus brought His own pressure, which constantly kept the devil off-balance and scrambling to react to Him. He knew God and His standing with Him, so it was only normal for Him to carry Himself as a spiritual winner.

When Jesus' time for ministry came, people recognized the kingdom as it was being introduced through the preaching of John the Baptist, again in the wilderness (another illustration of this world condition we find all find ourselves in). Miraculously, vast multitudes of people even travelled out of the cities to hear this heavenly announcement of the Messiah's impending appearance. They traveled to find John in a remote location where he was baptizing and calling people to repentance on the Jordan River. Many repented of their own wayward spiritual conditions, pressing past their comfort zones, and into the promise of God's Kingdom about to come in power (Matthew 3). The Lord answered that movement with a movement of His own, the shock and awe of which we have never forgotten.

Getting God's Seed in Your Ground

Jesus started and stopped spiritual storms, introducing the way two kingdoms should continue to clash until He returns to consummate all things in God's eternal plan for planet Earth. He masterfully used this spiritual law of motion with its reciprocating effects, and taught us to continue doing the same as extensions of His work.

The most central explanation of His approach to overcoming evil with good, is found in the third, fourth, and fifth chapters of the gospel of Mark. You will notice that this teaching is both preceded and followed by lessons on the importance of dealing with Satan. This is extremely important for us to recognize when planning to bring a full heavenly response to our circumstances and communities—you must also know Satan will fight to ensure you are not successful.

Jesus first talks about the necessity of being strong, through unity of spirit, to defeat and bind the strong man who is coming to your house with bad intentions (Mark 3:22-30). He then outlines the principle of sowing and reaping, to ensure that we establish a secure kingdom environment around the property that God has given us, in anticipation of producing big results for Him (Mark 4:1-34). Jesus teaches us to recognize spiritual realities around us, move to enlarge God's territory in our lives and overcome the storms that our enemy would stir up to stop us from finishing our course (Mark 4:35-5:21). Receiving the seeds that God sows into our hearts is central to this overall process. I mentioned before how the kingdom was the overwhelming theme of Jesus' ministry.

He taught over forty parables to paint the picture of what that means to us. This parable is so important because He said it unlocks our understanding of all the others. You could say it is the very heart of Jesus' message that He does not want us to miss (Mark 4:13). Even though farming is the extremely slow side of spiritual motion, it is motion nonetheless, and describes the same process that we see in the faster example of a rocket being propelled to the sky. We can know what we are dealing with and how to make the most of it long before leaving the barn, just by understanding the potential of the seeds when we first put them into our ground.

"And He said to them, To you has been entrusted the mystery of the kingdom of God [that is, the secret counsels of God which are hidden from the ungodly]; but for those outside [of our circle] everything becomes a parable, in order that they may [indeed] look and look but not see and perceive, and may

hear and hear but not grasp and comprehend, lest haply they should turn again, and it [their willful rejection of the truth] should be forgiven them. [Isa. 6:9, 10; Matt. 13:13-15.] And He said to them, Do you not discern and understand this parable? How then is it possible for you to discern and understand all the parables?" **Mark 4:11-13 AMP**

The Lord boils it all down to two very important things with regard to the 3rd law of spiritual motion. First, Jesus specifically said the parable of the sower and the seeds reveals the deepest secrets of God's kingdom to those who want to know. Exactly what you put into it is what you can expect back, but like seeds in any good field, motion with God is rewarded on every level of effort, with a much greater yield than the initial input of energy. 'Opposite' in God's equation, is not limited to equal; it is thirty, sixty, and a hundredfold greater (Mark 4:20, 30-32). How important it is to make sure that He is a vital part of the spiritual equation in our towns and not just assume that all the right things will grow in and around us, just the way they should.

Second, what Jesus says in verse 12 is reiterated again in verse 34 for added emphasis. He purposefully didn't teach anything publicly without the use of analogy and metaphor, to disguise the heart of His message, from those with bad intentions. When it comes to the "Law of Sowing and Reaping" described here, the heart is the central issue governing the result. Notice that, by comparing verses 3-8 with verses 14-20, we clearly see how natural and spiritual results are similar in this parable. This is why I can make the same comparison with the laws of motion. Anything God made works according to godly principles, so the earth naturally works in accordance with spiritual laws

That means that any seed carries within it the potential to reproduce abundantly, and the ground it comes to rest in is equally important in determining how great the payoff actually is in the end. Spiritually speaking, that ground is the human heart, it is where Satan battles God for possession of men's souls. Since verse 13 tells us that this parable is the key to understanding every other parable

Jesus told, you might say it is also the cornerstone in a man's relationship with God, upon which His Kingdom is built. This is why Satan comes immediately and aggressively after what God sows toward a people or place. Satan tries to destroy God's Word three specific ways in an effort to stop it from penetrating the human heart with heavenly roots. When you see these activities happening in or around you, your family or your town, beware. God is about to do something, unless the heart of the matter gets damaged first.

The devil first tries to take God's Word by preventing it from echoing throughout our being, once we first hear it. If he can get us to forget the initial interest we showed when faith opened our ears, the devil can get in and out without us realizing we even had the experience. He takes the seed before it has time to penetrate the deepest level of a life or group. If he is unsuccessful with that tactic, he then tries to harden the ground around our human hearts after the Word makes its initial entry there. What does it really say about a town when the people there are interested in everything but the Lord?

The second process here manifests as afflictions, persecutions, and offenses. If Satan can eliminate the natural water from the ground surrounding the heavenly seed, he can kill it before it springs up. A spiritual climate waters the soul of a society, especially where the ground tends to be hard to start with. If you were the enemy, wouldn't your second strategy against God be to throw up a smokescreen at any cost, once the seed had been received by people? At this stage he uses multiple forms of harassment against us until our hearts hurt too much to care about reproducing.

The third scheme is the last line of defense. After we have heard and received what God is saying to us with some emotional investment, and have shown the resilience to not give into assaults on our happiness, the devil has to go to 'Code Red.' This is when he magnifies the other things that we care about, in an effort to squeeze God out. There are so many thorny places in the old nature section of the human heart that most of us are still susceptible at this stage to the tug on all those areas that the world system we live in, naturally provides. Cares, money, and lusts beg to be fed, but if we resist the temptation to yield to these things, the potential inside God's words to produce Kingdom-level results, is only a matter of time.

In the end, Jesus says the same thing a few different ways. "The Kingdom of God works like a man sowing seed into the ground." It works like the smallest seed, a mustard seed, being put through the motions of growth. Even that little seed when mixed with faith produces a tree large enough for the enemy to sit in the shade of, wondering how he is going to stop all the other seeds that that tree is producing. For all our talk about this enemy, when we move with God His way, nothing can stop our sure advance. It is simply a matter of letting God have a bigger measure of our own lives to work His investment plans through. Our movements in Him will come back, good measure, pressed down, shaken together and running over—anywhere (Luke 6:38; Mark 11:25).

God's Law of the Land is what really provides justice here in the spiritually lawless wilderness of this world we are settling. As we are about to see, it is the plurality of believers, working together, which sets the right atmosphere and lays the groundwork for heavenly productions to be cultivated here on Earth. Never underestimate the power of a seed sown, and don't be afraid to sow your life as a seed for Him to grow. When Peter and John ran into trouble with the natural law in Acts 4:18-20, they did what we have to be willing to do today, invoke God's higher law—and keep taking land.

CHAPTER 8
Our Final Move

MAKING THIS LAW EVEN BIGGER

Twice between the sixth and ninth grades, I had the ultimate wake-up calls in my young life. As proof of how the human heart is so severely tipped in sin's direction, even near death experiences did not move me to answer God's call during this seven year period! In the meantime, my struggle to find myself during my elementary through high school life, transpired. I thank God for His patience every time I think back on those formative years. Without the goodness and grace of God, none of us, especially a kid born on the wrong side of the tracks like me, can fight, let alone win the kind of spiritual battle being described in this book.

Right in the middle of my sixth grade year, just before that first big fight I lost my identity in, I was diagnosed with probable bone cancer of the hip and initially given an ominous prognosis. It only took seven days of strict bed rest, thinking I was going to die, before the doctors at the clinic I went to, discovered the 'cancer' was only a shadow on my x-ray! Then just a few days before my fifteenth birthday, I was involved in a serious car accident which nearly killed me for real. It took several months to recover from serious surgery to stop internal bleeding, remove the pieces of my exploded spleen and repair a failing kidney. During that time I sunk into a discouraging place in my heart that made catching up in my school studies even harder to do.

These things contributed to my uphill struggle in life that was very real and dark, yet hard to explain to anyone else. I did not understand myself until years after the Lord brought me fully through it and out of it, to follow Him on the other side. I remember several 'coincidental' encounters during my car accident recovery, where people would approach me and say things like, "God saved your life for a reason." However, the better I felt, the less inclined I was to pay much attention to those passing people and their comments, but eventually they all added up. It took some time for God to work me through a process to get His desired response from me.

The forces of good and evil are battling for people like you and me every day, who also do not realize the stakes involved. In my position then, as a mostly unchurched, undisciplined, stubborn-headed, independent child of the '70's with a big chip on my shoulder, this spiritual war was hard to recognize. Yet somehow, here I am. I haven't really changed all that much. I'm still in the midst of the battle between good and evil, but now for other lives. Some people won't relate to me, but maybe I'm just the kind of guy who needs to say these things, especially from the viewpoint of living through the events in places like Newtown and Columbine? The religion of today is not going to bind Satan's hands and the political landscape isn't going to push us toward a return to the kind of spirituality that has revived America many times in her past. We need an awakening like I did as a teenager, so that we can fight for that higher sense of destiny that we feel in our hearts.

Somebody else could probably say this better, but I have something to say. My life story is one of struggling to come to God and then struggling thereafter, to understand why so many people seem to stop short of the spiritual line that the world needs Christians to cross. Believers are the best answer for evil on any day because they represent Jesus. I am one person that God is sending to say to you, "God has saved your life for a reason." Somebody around you needs the transfer of spiritual life that He wants to impart to you.

Laying Down the Law of the Spirit

Jesus got my attention a few years ago when I reread a rhetorical question that He asked, after using the example of a desperate widow's approach to an unjust judge. That question sums up all of the moves people can make to get God moving in their lives. In this final chapter, I want to remind you of the principles we have covered and the package that God put them in for maximum success in helping a hurting, dying world.

"Then the Lord said, Listen to what the unjust judge says! And will not [our just] God defend and protect and avenge His elect (His chosen ones), who cry to Him day and night? Will He defer them and delay help on their behalf? I tell you, He will defend and protect and avenge them speedily. However, when the Son of Man comes, will He find [persistence in] faith on the earth?" Luke 18:6-8 AMP

What the unjust judge in this parable said was, "Yes!" Although he did not fear God nor respect people, he relented to the pressure created by one poor, mistreated widow who was willing to keep 'drawing near' until she got what she needed! By taking the trouble to cause him trouble, this little lady received the reaction she wanted. Trouble in life can either cause us to quit, or it can put faith and prayer into motion together to get impossible answers. God is a just Judge, who loves to give good gifts to His children. Jesus didn't say He might help us, He said He would see to it *speedily.* The widow's example is the prevailing law of God's land!

So let's recap our 3 Spiritual Laws of Motion:

• When 'Murphy's Law' comes into play, take the trouble to draw on the '*Law of the Spirit of Life"* found in Christ Jesus. It lifts us above sin and death's destruction.

• When the 'Law of the Jungle' threatens your family, use the *'Law of Faith'* in prayer to do more than survive. It connects us to the King of Kings and moves mountains to enforce His rule.

• Employ the 'Law of God's Land,' the '*Law of Growing Returns'* to keep getting results in the spirit realm. It is the foundational law of God's Kingdom, the basis of all cause and effect.

We are also packaging these spiritual motions into 6 easy steps to take, in case anyone loses their way in the process:

- STEP #1 – Step back and look at the spiritual realities in and around your life. Choose to 'want to know' what you may not have been comfortable finding out.

- STEP #2 - Step away from the temptation to move the wrong way. Look evil in the eyes and choose the goodness of God's direction for you, your family and your town.

- STEP #3 - Step up and address your opportunity to change the playing field or reverse spiritual momentum. Find your 'waggle' so you can make your move.

- STEP #4 - Step forward and take your best shot at connecting with God and what He puts in front of you. Make a difference by forcing the right issues.

- STEP #5 - Step out and expect the results that God promises. Give Him the time and space to move in your world, so what comes back will pack an eternal punch. Become a carrier of knockout power.

The Equalizer

There is only one more step to take for anyone serious about using the spiritual law of motion and releasing God's goodness to overcome evil in our world. We have to move together.

- STEP #6 - Step through the door of God's Church. Engage in the corporate body that He has authorized to shut every door that hell tries to open in your community.

Our final move is to step completely 'through' the door that is Jesus Christ and take your place in His collective sheepfold. This may be the simplest principle of all but if it were as easy as it sounds, every Christian would already be doing it. Statistics show instead that although more people on our planet than ever, call themselves 'Christian', believers are increasingly more independent of one another in their approach to faith.

"So Jesus said again, I assure you, most solemnly I tell you, that I Myself am the Door for the sheep. All others who came [as such] before Me are thieves and robbers, but the [true] sheep did not listen to and obey them. I am the Door; anyone who enters in through Me will be saved (will live). He will come in and he will go out [freely], and will find pasture. The thief comes only in order to steal and kill and destroy. I came that they may have and enjoy life, and have it in abundance (to the full, till it overflows). I am the Good Shepherd, The Good Shepherd risks and lays down His [own] life for the sheep. [Psalm 23.] John 10:7-11 AMP

The word 'church' in the New Testament only really means a unified group of people, called out into a public forum, for the purposes of the Lord. In fact, this word should never have been translated as 'church' in English. The proper term would have been more appropriately translated as *the call*, because that is what we are summoned to: joint faith that reflects our individual trust in God. Church, like a lot of things today, has been dumbed down in modern society. The devil has worked this into a genius strategy to ensure that most godly people won't be able to find answers, but will experience overwhelming hurt and disappointment and slowly lose virtually all power to prevent the spread of wickedness in their spheres of influence.

Jesus died to be our door for a much bigger purpose than to save millions of people so that they can do whatever they feel is in their own best interests. Where's the power in that? When you watch the 'interfaith' memorial events which follow our tragedies today, it is hard to imagine anyone wanting to follow the motley cast of religious personalities that our towns often parade before a grief-stricken community. Jesus died for more than just to become an optional spiritual figure that people can take or leave. He's the only option, take Him or leave yourself to all the other bad choices that the world's version of religion has to offer.

"Simon Peter answered, 'You are the Messiah, the Son of the living God.' Jesus replied, 'You are blessed, Simon son of

John, because my Father in heaven has revealed this to you. You did not learn this from any human being. Now I say to you that you are Peter (which means 'rock') and upon this rock (which means 'large rock') I will build my church, and all the (gates) powers of hell will not conquer it. And I will give you the keys of the Kingdom of Heaven. Whatever you forbid on earth will be forbidden in heaven, and whatever you permit on earth will be permitted in heaven.'" **Matthew 16:16-19 NLT (parenthesis mine)**

The true Church on the other hand, still stands as the prevailing spiritual force on earth, able to overcome the very 'gates' of hell. It is noteworthy that these two words, 'gates' and 'doors' are synonyms, often used interchangeably in scripture. Jesus is the door then that slams the gate on the devil. We already established how He won that victory in his death, burial and resurrection and how He carries it out through the strength that He imparts to those who put faith in His blood sacrifice. But how does He carry it out? Surprisingly, by having divided Himself into millions of little carriers of heavenly authority! One only has to reread the prayers that Paul prayed for groups of believers like the church in Ephesus:

"And [so that you can know and understand] what is the immeasurable and unlimited and surpassing greatness of His power in and for us who believe, as demonstrated in the working of His mighty strength, which He exerted in Christ when He raised Him from the dead and seated Him at His [own] right hand in the heavenly [places], not only in this age and in this world, but also in the age and the world which are to come. And He has put all things under His feet and has appointed Him the universal and supreme Head of the church [a headship exercised throughout the church], [Ps. 8:6.] Which is His body, the fullness of Him Who fills all in all [for in that body lives the full measure of Him Who makes everything complete, and Who fills everything everywhere with Himself]. **Ephesians 1:19-23 AMP**

That verse alone is worth the price of any Bible. In fact, I advocate just taking the simple little six-chapter book of Ephesians from our New Testament, and rereading it until what it really says dawns on us. When we do, it begins to automatically separate our understanding totally from what passes for "church" today. The beautiful thing is that when we believe that God is using us together as a corporate expression of Jesus Himself, holding all the same power to act the same way that He did as one man, it starts uniting us with a sense of restored living spirituality...the kind that made Jesus so interesting.

Five times in Ephesians, we find that phrase that you just read, "heavenly places," being repeated. God leaves breadcrumb trails like this in scripture so we can find our way home to real Christianity when we get lost. This one here, leads us back home to the heavenly realm, that spiritual place where everything originates, both good and evil. God the Father works from there (Ephesians 1:3). Jesus Christ's seat of authority as King of Kings is there (Ephesians 1:20). We are seated in authority with Him there (Ephesians 2:6). Our enemy is there getting a lesson on how wise God is, by being forced to watch the church operate in the way I am describing (Ephesians 3:10). We are supposed to be actively wrestling with satanic powers there, dressed in God's own armor, praying with perseverance (Ephesians 6:11).

Paul said it best in speaking to a group of intellectuals at Athens. Quoting one of their own Greek philosophers, he unknowingly was telling the whole future world to come, how God is not unknown. Paul knew He was the only God, the One who engages us to live by the spiritual laws of motion.

"For in Him we live, and move, and have our being;" Acts 17:28 KJV

Paul was one of those guys that God called to show the rest of us how it's done. He wrote 13 or 14 epistles in the New Testament, modeled the message of the Gospel in the way it is to be expressed and individually taught us how to operate locally as the global Church of the living God. This is the same guy that is responsible for establishing those seven churches you read about in the final Bible book of Revelation. He is THE authority on 'church' because God anointed him to see it as no other early apostle did. Even Peter, the one Jesus first promised the Kingdom's keys to, referred us to Paul:

"...even as our brother Paul also wrote to you according to the spiritual insight given him, speaking of this as he does in all of his letters. There are some things in those [epistles of Paul] that are difficult to understand, which the ignorant and unstable twist and misconstrue to their own utter destruction, just as [they distort and misinterpret] the rest of the Scriptures." **2 Peter 3:15-16 AMP**

Paul demonstrated the power of spiritual motion by learning to focus all of his energy into the knowledge of Christ. Every time he entered a city, he did so as an apostle on an assignment to take territory for the Kingdom of Heaven (1 Corinthians 2:1-5). He knew from Jesus' own example that if he measured his ability by the promised power of God, his own weaknesses would actually contribute to a release of God's very glory resting upon his own life (2 Corinthians 12:9). He also knew the exponential power of unity promised to the children of Israel and how it applied to the believers working together as Christ's body (Deuteronomy 32:30). Paul was a spiritual Newton on steroids! If the church is the body of Christ, then he knew the power of it, even in smaller local sections, was as unlimited as Jesus Himself.

Intensity in Ten Cities

After Jesus taught the parable of the seed in Mark chapter four, He didn't even let the sun go down before taking a ship to the opposite side of the Sea of Galilee. This is interesting to me because of the lesson about equal and opposite reactions it teaches. What possessed Jesus to cross diagonally across the lake from Capernaum to Gadara to confront a possessed man? Maybe it was the spiritual insight about how freedom on the 'other side', could somehow equate to a greater move of God's spirit on the side where He based His ministry? There was something important about the

120

positioning of this man in the spirit realm for the Lord to take such aggressive action.

It was an opportunity to emphasize the importance of the law of sowing and reaping, in living color. Satan has a strategy in place and Jesus is God's answer to thwart it, as usual. Before his little armada made it, a 'coincidental' storm just happened to arise and fill the boat with water. I have always loved knowing that Jesus was a heavy sleeper in such situations; He was upset that they even woke Him up! When he got up, He just used the power of binding and loosing promised to this 'church', of which He was building a few disciples at a time. Jesus then called them out for not using their faith when they had the opportunity to practice being who He had called them to be.

Incidentally, 'Gadara' was a part of the tribal 'Gergashite' territory, originally given to Abraham and his *seed*- a direct reference to Christ (Genesis 15:15-20; Galatians 3:16). It was a region making up $1/7^{th}$ of the Canaanite nation that God had ordered the Israelites to invade under Joshua's leadership. If nothing else, this place belonged to Jesus in the spirit realm, so He was coming for what was His. The spiritual freedom of a man there was part of God's new covenant plan and was going to have an exponential effect. Jesus cast at least 2,000 demons out of one crazy man and sent him into the ten city region called 'Decapolis', to tell the story. The result was one crazy revival all around that lake! Back in Capernaum, miracles broke out as soon as Jesus returned, as the faith of many seemed to just rise (Mark 5:21-43). Within two chapters, we read of the same thing happening in the Decapolis, with the crowds getting so big that Jesus resorted to supernaturally feeding thousands!

This is the Law of Spiritual Motion in action. It may seem too good to be true but that is exactly what we possess together as Jesus' church to distribute...these were real people and places! Jesus knew the positioning of all heavenly powers and the potential of even one man full of God's Spirit, to disrupt Satan's kingdom. When He recognized a spiritual 'legion' strategically placed in God's way by the adversary, He simply wrestled it out of the way by allowing the

Holy Spirit to move Him in the right direction. Whatever He permitted on earth was permitted in the heavens and whatever He forbade here was forbidden there. That's how the keys work when He, and now we, carry them.

"When the Jews made a man a doctor of the law, they put into his hand the key of the closet in the temple where the sacred books were kept, and also tablets to write upon; signifying, by this, that they gave him authority to teach, and to explain the scriptures to the people. -Martin." Adam Clarke's Bible Commentary on Matthew 16:19.

We need not consult any other advice 'higher' than the Bible for dealing with evil in our cities. Before Jesus rose from the dead to manage all things from the throne of God, He instructed His followers to wait in Jerusalem until God clothed them with the power of the Holy Spirit. They did not have any further insight, so they simply let the law of spiritual motion take its course. Not knowing what else to do to engage God's plan, they made themselves available during these ten days by praying. Once they connected with God's timing, the Holy Spirit rushed into their room and pushed them out into their city like a mighty wind (Acts 2). The result was an increased ability to influence the people around them, who just happened to be gathered from around the known world that day. Ten days of prayer has turned into two thousand years of power to turn this world up-side-down.

No Small Stir

Paul was an unlikely, but eventual result of those events which kept spreading Jesus' message further geographically and deeper culturally. At first a zealously religious man bent on destroying this new church, he became its chief proponent once the Lord knocked him off of his high horse. More than most, Paul knew the power of good and evil to work through a heart, intent on doing right. He learned that you needed more than faith built on your own abilities, you really needed to know your God. This is what separates Christianity from all other religions and it is why Paul could march into the darkest pagan cities of his day, to shake and awaken their citizens.

Ephesus is just one such city. Again, I encourage you to read the contents of the letter that Paul wrote to the church that he 'planted' there, by virtue of his movements in God. To get the most out of it however, you should also read how this man's actions created a famous reaction in that place. **Acts 19** tells the story of Paul's steps in spiritual motion. He too, identified places where 'strong men' in the spirit world were ruling outcomes from and he proceeded to wrestle with them for the blessings of God to come.

Charting Paul's actions are simple now that we know how spiritual momentum works:

1. He **backed up** and assessed the true situation. Paul didn't tend to go anywhere without God's leading. By taking this first step, He found a few good men to transfer the Holy Ghost to and an opportunity to speak into the Ephesian Jewish community in the local synagogue. (verses 1-7)

2. He **moved away** from the temptation to stop when persecution arose from his own fellow Jewish religious ranks. This step afforded him the opportunity to separate those who believed from those who really believed. (verses 8-9)

3. He **addressed his situation** by moving those true disciples into an environment where they could focus on the Lord and become the 'church.' This was the Ephesian 'waggle.' (verses 9-10)

4. He **hit them with his best shot,** pouring everything he had into their lives for an extended period of time. (verse 10)

5. He **got the results** that he needed and much, much more! 'Special miracles' were an unexpected spiritual reaction in this case, which propelled the city into a frenzy of spiritual warfare. (Acts 19:11- 20:1)

Ephesus was another key city in a region. Paul was a key man in God's heavenly based Kingdom. These two things go together to create what the Bible calls 'apostolic ministry.' This is when someone is called to go somewhere and do some things that have not been done before. Today, we need a few more of these and few less 'pastors' running around doing all of the same things that somebody else has already done, somewhere else. It takes the fun out of Christianity and makes us immature and unimpressive...especially in the spirit realm.

Check Your Doors

The final thing I want to say is also found in final chapter of Ephesians. The result of every big movement that God makes, should be a powerful group of people who keep moving together for Him. He multiplies His army through every spiritual connection and transfer made along the way. It started with Jesus and continued through men like Paul to create centers of ongoing spiritual activity, wherever they went. There is a letter to the Ephesians in our Bibles because Ephesus was one of those centers.

Paul told us the secret to his success himself in 2 Corinthians 10:4. Spiritual 'strongholds' can be pulled down in and around our lives, if we learn to use the spiritual weapons that God has placed at our disposal. They are not natural, we do not fight on a human battlefield. We wrestle for human beings lives in the spirit, casting down things which Satan has worked hard to replace God with, in people's minds. Every culture on the planet is filled with such customs and the enemy works through them to inflict damage upon whole groups of people.

As I said before, the Church is the answer. It is God's new culture, equipped with His kind of thinking, imaginations, and customs. It is the result of His heavenly door swinging open in Jesus and it is the door into this world that He uses most to make His moves. We are where every spiritual law of motion gets magnified and the exponential power of God is intensified. For every move one of us can make, two of us can make it ten times stronger (Matthew 18:19-

20; Deuteronomy 32:30). The 'singularity' of God's technology has overtaken mankind long ago in the form of the Church.

We must protect the space between us and God and the spaces between ourselves for God, if we want to stop evil in the spaces around us. The church today has lost its identity, but we can bring it back even if we have to do it one city at a time. There are many examples of God's people working together in their towns today to restore spiritual order. Crime drops, opportunities increase and hope abounds in some of the most unlikely places, when we love God enough to love each other. We can open the doors of the real church again, if even two or three of us in any one place start agreeing with God to do so (Matthew 18:15-20).

(for examples of transformed towns see: http://www.transformourworld.org/en/itn/international-transformation-network)

"A final word; Be strong in the Lord and in his mighty power. Put on all of God's armor so that you will be able to stand firm against all strategies of the devil...so you will be able to resist the enemy in the time of evil. Then after the battle you will be standing firm." **Ephesians 6:10-13 NLT**

Paul wrote this letter to the whole Ephesian church, therefore, its contents are meant to be taken in a plural sense before we extract individual promises. It is no coincidence that he finished it by reminding them to not rest on the victories of their past, which as we discussed, were many. He emphasizes the need to stand together against the devil and his evil strategies. We are to be vigilant as soldiers, wearing specific attributes of God, which when used in the spirit of prayer, will repel advances by the dark side of the heavenly places we operate in. You might say these pieces of armor represent those spaces which must be protected between heaven and earth, God and His people, and among believers.

Paul's final words were, "be strong in the Lord." He wanted this particular church to recognize the importance of continuing to stand in a position of representing the Lord. The Church is likened to many things in scripture. We are God's garden, His sheepfold, bride, mysterious heavenly plan, school, and most important to our discussion, His body and temple or building. As indicated here, we are also an army, broken down into many pieces of one whole battle plan. You could say that each local church is like a fortress or stronghold for God in their region.

So in the end, we need to protect what we have, to ensure that we stand our ground against evil and keep our skies open to God's blessings. Maybe the simplest way to close this chapter is by leaving you with Paul's simplified plan to keep the House of God secure so the heavenly power will flow at its highest levels. Use this list of armor as a way to check for openings for the enemy in your life. Is every door secured the way God prescribes? More importantly, are the spiritual church doors locked to prevent the intrusion of evil? If God can't get to me, and the believers in any given place can't get to him, we have a problem.

It's time to put this book into action and use it to reach the world for good. If you are a believer, start by going around and checking the doors that Paul said could create enough spiritual movement to awaken an Ephesus. Keeping them open is what shuts the devil down. God's armor gives us the strength to enter our battles already victorious. Standing on what Jesus has done we will wrestle every outcome away from the enemy together in prayer!

<u>Final Checklist</u>:

- **TRUTH - Step back and be honest.**
- **RIGHT STANDING WITH GOD - Step away from sin.**
- **THE GOSPEL - Step up and embrace the message.**
- **FAITH - Step forward and believe.**
- **SALVATION - Step out and expect God's results.**
- **SPIRIT - Step into God's supernatural reality.**

"Stand your ground, putting on the belt of truth and the body armor of God's righteousness. For shoes, put on the peace

that comes from the Good News so that you will be fully prepared. In addition to all of these, hold up the shield of faith to stop the fiery arrows of the devil. Put on salvation as your helmet, and take the sword of the Spirit, which is the word of God. Pray in the Spirit at all times and on every occasion. Stay alert and be persistent in your prayers for all believers everywhere." Ephesians 6:14-18 NLT

AFTERWORD

THE HIGHEST LAW OF ALL

God cares about people's 'whys', today. That is why He has worked hard to give people like you, the heavenly answers that many are beginning to realize they need. So be courageous and take a good hard look at 'what' is really happening all around you. There is a very real and present danger, lurking even in places as seemingly out-of-the-way as Newtown, Connecticut. Our spiritual enemy can only be moved when identified, engaged and wrestled with in prayer, until Christ's victory over him is enforced where you live.

Most people know something about the power of love, even when they haven't experienced much of it in life. The Bible calls love the greatest thing of all, the essence of Who God is (1John 4:8, 16; 1 Corinthians 13). This is why people respond so well as a whole in times of crisis and tragedy. We all have a big deposit of love inside, whether we know or act on it or not, because we were created by love. What you may not know is that it is also a law – the highest law of all:

"If indeed you [really] fulfill the royal Law in accordance with the Scripture, You shall love your neighbor as [you love] yourself, you do well. [Leviticus 19:18.]" **James 2:8 AMP**

Take it from those who followed Jesus, love is the excellence of His way. When it comes to stopping evil, this is the ultimate weapon that we must put into motion in our lives. Love is what the devil does not have and cannot control. Every time we use it as our motivation, we release God and open doors that Hell cannot close. Even a purely natural love is powerful but the God kind is truly out-of-this-world. It has a selfless quality that can only be found in the heart of God, which enables us to treat people in a God-kind of way. All of our motions have to be governed by love.

I would not feel right finishing this book without doing two important things. First, I remind you to bathe everything you do in love. It is the law of royalty and liberty in God's kingdom so if we want the spiritual law of motion to work for us, it has to be channeled through hearts of love.

"But if you look carefully into the perfect law that sets you free, and if you do what it says and don't forget what you heard, then God will bless you for doing it." **James 1:25 NLT**

Second, I remind you again, how serious this subject is. God is going to hold everyone accountable one day. The Bible says the criteria of His judgment will be based on how we responded to Christ and whether we carried out His directives to respond to each other. The bottom line is that we will be rewarded based on how we did things in this life with regard to good and evil.

"For we must all stand before Christ to be judged. We will each receive whatever we deserved for the good or evil we have done in this earthly body." **2 Corinthians 5:10 NLT**

When Jesus came the first time, he wept over the city of Jerusalem because of their refusal to realize the timing of their visitation and embrace His love (Luke19:44). Their mentality and movements were so out of sync with the God they professed to worship that when He came and walked in their midst, they did not even recognize Him! If it can happen to them, it can easily happen to us. In fact, it will happen to many according to Jesus' own words (Matthew 24:12). God was willing to embrace His people then and He is just as willing now, but what will He find to work with on our end? He is looking for that connector called 'faith', which only works when it is connected to love (Luke 18:8; Galatians 5:6).

Jesus loved them deeply but He also warned them explicitly about the penalty for disregarding a love so great.

"O Jerusalem, Jerusalem, the city that kills the prophets and stones God's messengers! How often I have wanted to gather your children together as a hen protects her chicks beneath her wings, but you wouldn't let me. And now, look, your house is abandoned and desolate. For I tell you this, you will never see me again until you say, Blessings on the one who comes in the name of the Lord!" **Matthew 23:37-39**

The aftermath of His predictions in Matthew 24 and Luke 21 about Jerusalem are truly frightening. Because they did not take place until nearly 40 years later, Christians often forget to take them into consideration when serving God today. Just so we won't make the same mistake, I remind you of them here. Jesus said there would be signs to look up and see for Jewish believers then and again when He returned a second time. Much of what we see today could be indicative of His soon return.

How important is this for us to consider? It may help to consider first what literally happened around Jerusalem in the years leading up to its destruction in 70 A.D.:

"Still further, Jesus Himself prophesied. "...that false Christs should arise, and should deceive many; that there should be earthquakes and famines, and fearful sights in heaven, and wars and rumors of wars, and great tribulation, such as was not since the beginning of the world, nor ever should be; and that Jerusalem should be compassed with armies; and that a trench should be cast round about it; and that one stone of the temple should not be left upon another; and that the Jews should be carried captive among all nations." Josephus verifies all these predictions to the letter. He was an eyewitness and a Jew, and nothing can be more striking than the comparison of his history with the prophecy. He tells of "fearful sights and great signs from heaven"; that "before sunsetting, chariots, and troops of soldiers in their armor, were seen running about among the clouds." "At the feast of Pentecost, as the priests were going by night into the inner court of the Temple, they felt a quaking, and heard a great noise, and, after that, they heard the sound as of a multitude, saying, "Let us depart hence.""

Tacitus, a Roman historian, also says, "There were many prodigies presignifying their ruin which was not averted by all the sacrifices and vows of that people. Armies were seen fighting in the air with brandished weapons. A fire fell upon the Temple from the clouds. The doors of the Temple were suddenly opened. At the same time there was a loud voice saying that the gods were removing, which was accompanied with a sound as of a multitude going out. All which things were supposed, by some to portend great calamities. "

Josephus further says that "no other city ever suffered such miseries; nor was there ever a generation more fruitful in wickedness from the beginning of the world. ...In reality it was God who condemned the whole nation and turned every course that was taken for their preservation to their destruction. . . . The multitudes of those who perished exceeded all the destructions that man or God ever brought upon the world."

Famine did its slow but dreadful work so that women were known to eat their own children, just as Moses said they would do, fifteen hundred years before. The prophecy of Christ that not one stone of the Temple should be left upon another, was literally fulfilled. The Jews were carried into captivity among all nations..." Mark Hopkins, 1844 (Hopkins' Evidences, pp. 322-324.)

Jesus was serious when he said things. Be smart enough to take what He said seriously. If you do, you will not only save yourself but many of those around you. There are so many signs today – people see all kinds of things in the skies, we've just never stopped to think that much of it could be heavenly warfare going on in the spirit realm. Be careful which things you attach yourself to. I like that the Lord's final words were words of motion. He said "watch", "be ready", "stay faithful" so you won't get caught off guard and allow your house to be broken down (Matthew 24:42-51). Jesus loves you!

My Dream - March 20, 2013

The dream began as I was approaching a bridge in New York City from the west, looking up to the center of the bridge through all its metal girders out into the open sky. I could not see the other side because of the raised arc of the design, only the unfolding roadway as I proceeded forward. At this point I realized that I was actually escorting two old high school friends and my youngest daughter across this bridge. The overall feeling was very relaxed but as we advanced toward the center of the bridge, I began to notice that the conditions around us had become subtly turbulent. The wind was blowing strongly and the water underneath this bridge was jumping up above its railings on either side. It was as if not everyone else realized what was happening, but our height coupled with these conditions, suddenly made me aware of just how dangerous things had turned in such a small amount of time. Sensing the need to remain calm, I continued acting relaxed and unfazed by the circumstances. This helped eventually bring our destination back in perspective as we headed down the other side. During this entire time I really felt sure of where we were going but it was also like I had never been there before. My purpose seemed to be making sure the flow of things did not cause people to get caught up in the things around us, before we arrived at our destination. As the other side came into view, I realized that we needed to find a restaurant in which to eat. We found an upscale place and the dream ended with the owners of the restaurant telling us that they had been expecting our arrival and had a job offer suited to my daughter's abilities. Since she enjoys cooking, it seemed surprising yet perfectly normal. Upon awakening I found myself saying, "that was the Kosciuszko Bridge."

Knowing that God was trying to tell me something but that I would have to search out this mystery, I began to do some digging. In researching the Kosciuszko bridge, I discovered that it crosses over the "Newtown Creek" in between Brooklyn and Queens. This obviously means a lot to me and by now it should be starting to mean just as much to you. The events of 12-14-12 in Newtown, CT though tragic, are very indicative of the escalating turbulence and danger in our current world. It is real and we have to face it, to cross over it with courage and get to where we are supposed to go in these last days. What's more is that the Kosciuszko bridge is widely considered to be the most dangerous bridge in New York City, therefore it is due to be 'rebuilt' in the days ahead. It reminds me of God's Church. It too is being more than restored…it is being

133

rebuilt to better reflect the Kingdom of Heaven and to streamline the harvest that God is collecting from the cities of this world. Choose to be a radical, revolutionary for that kingdom. Wake up, this is your bridge! Be one that God can send to the other side; a part of the real church that overcomes all adversity and becomes THE answer for the dangers of this age. There is an important meal waiting for us, and those we transfer God's life to, on the other side! (Revelation 19:9)

WORKS CITED

Author n.a. Connecticut Museum Quest. n.p. Web. 20 November 2013.

Author Unknown. "Law of the Land". Wikipedia. 18 November 2013. web. 20 November 2013.

Author Unknown. "Newton's Toolbox".Ohio State University. n.d. Web. 20 November 2013.

Author Unknown. "Standard Operating Procedure". Wikipedia. 29 October 2013. web. 20 November 2013.

Batman is a registered trademark of DC Comics, New York, NY 10019

Big Think. "Michio Kaku: This Super Camera Captures What is Beyond Human Comprehension". Online video clip. *Youtube*. Youtube. 22 February 2012. web. 20 November 2013.

Citro, Joseph.. Weird New England. New York: Sterling; First Edition, September 25, 2005. Print.

Collins English Dictionary – Complete and Unabridged, copyright HarperCollins Publishers 1991, 1994,   1998, 2000, 2003

Collins, Suzanne. *The Hunger Games*. New York: Scholastic Press, 2008. Print

Finney, C. G. *The CHARACTER, CLAIMS, AND Practical Work-ings of FREEMASONARY,* Cincinnat: Western Tract and Book Society. 1869

Flynn, David. *Temple at the Center of Time*. Crane MO 65633: "Official Disclosure" A division of Anomalos Publishing House, 2008.

Klein, John and Spears, Adam. *Lost in Translation, Rediscovering the Roots of the Hebrew Faith*, Selah Publishing Group, LLC, Tennessee

LeBlanc, Curtis. Satan Service. Church of Satan. n.d. Web. 20 November 2013.

More, Thomas. *Utopia.* n.p. 1516. Print.

Nations, Jim and Romero, Karen. "Can We Find the Roots of Free Masonry in the Bible?". *Frances and Friends. 2013*

Newton, I. General Scholium. Translated by Motte, A. 1825. *Newton's Principia: The Mathematical Principles of Natural Philosophy.* New York: Daniel Adee, 501.

Pingel, Linda. "Early History of the Town of New Hartford." Town of New Hartford. n.p. 30 May 2000. web. 20 November 2013.

Raiders of the Lost Ark. Steven Spielberg. Paramount Pictures, 1981. Film.

Rocky. John G. Avildsen. United Artists. 1976. Film.

Strong, James. "Reprinted by permission. *Strong's Exhaustive Concordance of the Bible*, 1995, Thomas Nelson Inc. Nashville, Tennessee. All rights reserved."

The Dark Knight Rises. Christopher Nolan. Warner Bros. Pictures. 2012. Film

Everyday Preparation for Jesus' Return

365 Ways to Stay Ready

Rocky Veach

WWW.ROCKYVEACH.COM
WWW.ROCKYVEACH.ORG

Made in the USA
Charleston, SC
10 December 2013